DEDICATION

For my husband, Bradley, my biggest supporter and the only travel companion I'd have beside me on this journey of life.

GRAND STRAND BREWING COMPANY
819
GSB
GSB

CONTENTS

Music and Entertainment

Sports and Recreation

Shopping and Fashion

ACKNOWLEDGMENTS

They say it takes a village, and the same goes for gathering all the components to write a book like this. A big thanks goes to my family: my husband, Bradley, and my sons, Brady, Kipton, and Xander, who all helped me both scope my entries out in town over the course of a year and put up with my long days of writing. I'd also like to thank Visit Myrtle Beach, part of the Myrtle Beach Area Chamber of Commerce, for helping me with the photos for the book. Lastly, the restaurant and hospitality industries in Myrtle Beach are severely understaffed and overworked with the influx of clientele moving into the area, so a big thank-you to everyone in the service industry for taking care of my family of five when we are out and about. Thank you! I couldn't have done it without all of you in my corner!

DIRTY DON'S
OYSTER BAR
& GRILL
BOARDWALK
Paradise
General Store
N.Y.
STYLE PIZZA
THE SLICE
TRAVELER
ATM

PREFACE

I have lived in Myrtle Beach, South Carolina, for more than 20 years. It's a beautiful place that millions of tourists consider a vacation destination for a week or two in the summer, but I get to call it home. And I realize how lucky I am to do so. Writing this book has been a reminder of all of the special places and activities I've discovered over the years with my husband or my three sons—a love letter, if you will, to those memories and to making new ones.

The Myrtle Beach area is part of what is called "The Grand Strand," a 60-mile stretch of coastline that runs from Little River to the north to Georgetown to the south, and I've included these areas in this book as well. Myrtle Beach has picked up some other not-so-nice nicknames in the past, like "Redneck Riviera" or "Dirty Myrtle," but we've taken it on the chin. In fact, our area has most recently become one of the hottest, fastest-growing real estate markets in the country.

My goal with this book is to let those new to the area know—and to refresh the memory of the locals—why Myrtle Beach is continuously ranked as the place to be, and what you need to do here before you die. Over my decades as a writer, I've covered countless people doing great things and places to see and do in shorter features, but never written a full book dedicated to the wonders of Myrtle Beach. Until now. I hope you enjoy this, essentially, tribute to my home.

Life is short; time is fast; enjoy it to the fullest.

Ashley Daniels

Seafood Tower at RipTydz

FOOD AND DRINK

SHUCK OYSTERS
AT NANCE'S

September through April is oyster season in our coastal waters, swimming with these shellfish delicacies. During those months, make your way to Nance's Creekfront Restaurant & Oyster Roast for a bucket of steamed oysters hauled over to tables equipped with a hole in the middle for the shucked shell discards. This mainstay of Murrells Inlet has been serving local oyster roasts since 1967, known to have the largest shellfish lease in South Carolina and to harvest its own oysters daily. The interior decor, with its wood-paneled walls, is unapologetically outdated, but the waterfront views from any table are hands down the best in the inlet. On some days, early birds may even witness Nance's oyster harvesters trudging through the pluff mud, bringing in a load from the oyster beds clinging to the banks around the bend. At the end of every oyster season, the eco-friendly Nance's loads all the empty shells onto a barge and spreads them back into the oyster beds in the inlet to give birth to new oyster spawns.

4883 US 17 Business, Murrells Inlet, 843-651-2696
nancescreekfront.com

TIP

Dip the plump oyster muscle in a cup of warm, drawn butter, or pair it with a cracker slathered with cocktail sauce and Tabasco.

2

DIG INTO A BOWL
OF CHICKEN BOG

It may not look pretty, but chicken bog is a delicious northeast South Carolina staple that feeds the heart and soul. There's even a festival in our area named after it! The one-pot dish, called chicken bog because the chicken gets "bogged down" in the rice, is a blend of rice, chicken, and sausage. Dating back to as early as the 1920s, chicken bog used to be cooked up in a cast-iron washpot over an open wood fire for the crowds gathering tobacco near the end of August. Today, you can dig into a bowl of chicken bog served at several Southern soul food restaurants in the Myrtle Beach area or at the Loris Bog-Off Festival held in the small country town of Loris near the end of October each year. Always a big hit, the festival features a chicken bog cooking contest, live entertainment, and arts and crafts vendors.

3

LOAD UP
AT AN ALL-YOU-CAN-EAT FRIED SEAFOOD BUFFET

Myrtle Beach is laden with all-you-can-eat fried (also referred to as Calabash-style) seafood buffets. Named after a town located just north over the border in North Carolina, Calabash also refers to the style of preparation that coats fresh shrimp, fish, oysters, and more with a light batter, and then dropped into a hot fryer to crispy, salty, and light-golden brown deliciousness. Pair your seafood with a basket of Southern hush puppies, deep-fried balls of dough that can morph from sweet to savory.

While fried seafood is typically the star of the heated bins lining local buffets, you'll also find heaping piles of steamed crab legs, broiled or blackened seafood, plus a plethora of sides, salads, and desserts to suit your fancy. Just bring your patience, as these all-you-can-eat restaurants are hot spots for tourists over the summer, and your appetite!

BEST OF BUFFETS

Captain George's Seafood Restaurant
1401 29th Ave. N, Myrtle Beach, 843-916-2278
captaingeorges.com

Crabby Mike's
290 US 17 Business, Surfside Beach, 843-238-3524
crabbymikes.com

The Original Benjamin's Calabash Seafood
9593 N Kings Hwy., Myrtle Beach, 843-449-0821
originalbenjamins.com

Bennett's Calabash Seafood Buffet
9701 N Kings Hwy., Myrtle Beach, 843-449-7865
bennettscalabash.net

4

CATCH A SEAFOOD FESTIVAL
IN LITTLE RIVER

Little River is a quiet fishing village laden with history that's about 20 miles north of the more commercialized Myrtle Beach. Caught up in a slower pace of life, it's also known for fresh seafood, fishing charters, and serving as a host for annual seafood festivals. The World Famous Blue Crab Festival is first up on the weekend after Mother's Day, when you can feast on fresh local blue crab and seafood, listen to live beach music, and shop. Later in the year, the Little River Shrimp Fest takes over the town's waterfront in October. Shrimp and fresh local seafood are the stars of the show, along with two stages of live music and hundreds of arts and crafts vendors lining the waterfront on Mineola Avenue.

Mineola Ave., Little River
littlerivershrimpfest.org, bluecrabfestival.org

TIP

Because parking off Mineola Avenue is limited for these festivals, consider arriving by way of the *Sea Screamer* water taxi that commutes until 5 p.m. and is available out of Grande Harbour Marina at 4430 Kingsport Road, Little River. A $20 ticket per person includes a round trip aboard the *Sea Screamer*, admission to the festival, and parking at the marina.

5

CELEBRATE WITH STEAK
AT NEW YORK PRIME

Sure, seafood is the centerpiece of our table spreads here on the coast, but that doesn't mean our local chefs don't know their way around stellar cuts of USDA grade prime beef—on a luxury level. One standout Myrtle Beach steak house that fits the bill to make reservations for your special event: New York Prime.

New York Prime is an upscale, but cozy, steak house, reminiscent of old-school New York and well known by locals. Start with their classic Caesar or beefsteak tomatoes and onion salad drizzled with Brooklyn French dressing and oysters on the half shell. Follow that with the title role of any of Prime's cuts, from the petite filet to the strip to the porterhouse and more, all aged 28 days and prepared Pittsburgh-style with a charred exterior. Finish it with a side of lyonnaise and a slice of cheesecake shipped directly from the Big Apple.

405 28th Ave. N, Myrtle Beach, 843-448-8081
newyorkprime.com

6

TAKE A CRACK AT A SEAFOOD TOWER

ON THE ROOFTOP OF RIPTYDZ

RipTydz Oceanfront Grille & Rooftop Bar is my happy place. When you sit on the open-air rooftop dining area of this mega, multilevel venue right on the Myrtle Beach Boardwalk, you feel like you're on top of the world. Each floor of RipTydz has covered dining portions as well, with wide open windows that let the intoxicating sea breeze in, but the rooftop is my fave. What makes it even better? Having one of their fresh, chilled seafood towers on ice on the table in front of me. Choose your Tyde: there's the Low Tyde Tower stacked with a dozen raw oysters and a half pound of peel-and-eat shrimp; the High Tyde, one pound of little neck clams, a snow crab cluster, a half pound of pickled mussels, and one pound of peel-and-eat shrimp; or the RipTyde to share, consisting of a dozen raw oysters, a half pound of peel-and-eat shrimp, a whole one-pound live Maine lobster, Dungeness crab clusters, snow crab clusters, seared ahi tuna, and seared salmon.

1210 N Ocean Blvd., Myrtle Beach, 843-945-1204
riptydz.com

TIP

There's no need to worry about the scarce Ocean Boulevard parking. Take advantage of RipTydz's free valet!

7

LAP UP THE SHE CRAB SOUP

AT SEA CAPTAIN'S HOUSE

Sea Captain's House has survived the Myrtle Beach oceanfront since the 1940s, despite Hurricane Hazel damaging her supports under the front porch in 1954 and threats of high-rise hotels replacing her. The vacation beach cottage evolved from a guesthouse with nine guest rooms into the beloved restaurant it is today. There's not a bad seat in the house, indoors or alfresco on their oceanfront patio. There's also not a bad Southern dish on their breakfast, lunch, and dinner menus. One must-try is a bowl of Sea Captain's award-winning she crab soup. After a spoonful, you'll know why the dish is the restaurant's pride and joy, and why folks around here vote that it deserves an award year after year. Creamy, savory she crab soup is a classic Lowcountry dish stirred up with a blend of blue crab meat and sherry—and you'll want to lick the bowl clean.

3002 N Ocean Blvd., Myrtle Beach, 843-448-8082
seacaptains.com

GO BIG
AT BIG MIKE'S SOUL FOOD

Owner Mike Chestnut, aka "Big Mike," is the personality, heart, and soul of Big Mike's Soul Food, and you'll feel all those Southern hospitality vibes when you walk through the door of his place. Open since 2012, Big Mike's has been known for their cooked-to-order special meat 'n' three plates here in town and on a national scale, having recently been named by *Southern Living* as one of "Our Favorite Meat 'n' Threes" in the South. Meat choices are fried chicken, grilled chicken breast, fried pork chops, grilled pork chops, chopped sirloin, fried fish, grilled fish, fried livers, or fried gizzards. Pair that with any of their homemade sides: rice and gravy, mashed potatoes and gravy, collard greens, cabbage, baked mac and cheese, field peas, corn, candied yams, fried okra, potato salad, coleslaw, lima beans, pinto beans, or mustard greens.

Myrtle Beach born and raised, Chestnut learned the ropes from his mother at home and worked his way around local kitchens since age 12. Today, he runs Big Mike's with his wife and three children.

504 16th Ave. N, Myrtle Beach, 843-712-2048
bigmikessoulfood.net

9

DRINK YOUR WAY DOWN
THE MYRTLE BEACH BEER TRAIL

The beach's beer scene is serious! Since 2020, the number of local craft breweries has doubled (and more are in the works), so they all banded together to create the Myrtle Beach Beer Trail in 2023. Sip on the hoppy harvests from 10 of the area's best local breweries in this location-based digital passport, which includes a multimedia guide you can check into and earn prizes along the way. Tap into these trail highlights: Crooked Hammock Brewery, a massive venue in Barefoot Landing that offers a full-scale restaurant, kids' playground and lawn games, waterfront Tortuga Island gazebo bar, and large taproom serving tastings and tours; Tidal Creek Brewhouse in The Market Common area, featuring a dozen of their own brews (even a seltzer), a food café, indoor and outdoor seating, a taproom, a large backyard beer garden, and a dog run; New South Brewing, Myrtle Beach's original brewery in the heart of downtown (try the Dirty Myrtle Double IPA); and Grand Strand Brewing Company, or GSB, located in the newly renovated Nance Plaza with ocean views.

Crooked Hammock Brewery
4924 Hwy. 17 S, North Myrtle Beach, 843-962-7238
crookedhammockbrewery.com

Tidal Creek Brewhouse
3421 Knoles St., Myrtle Beach, 843-839-0959
tidalcreekbrewhouse.com

New South Brewing
1109 Campbell St., Myrtle Beach, 843-916-2337
newsouthbrewing.com

Grand Strand Brewing Company
819 N Kings Hwy., Myrtle Beach, 843-839-2801
grandstrandbrewing.com

For the trail: visitmyrtlebeach.com/beer

MUNCH
ON SHRIMP AND GRITS

The sweetheart of a Southern brunch, classic shrimp and grits has been cooked up in Lowcountry kitchens for the last 70 years. Fresh, local steamed shrimp are the stars of the dish, with stone-ground grits, or hominy, as the foundation. The rest of the ingredients that swim in shrimp and grits recipes in Myrtle Beach really vary by the chefs' tastes and cultural backgrounds, whether it's sautéing shrimp with onions and peppers or frying shrimp in bacon grease and then creating a shrimp gravy with just the right touch of seasonings. A few of my favorite spots around town for shrimp and grits are Blueberry's Grill, which adds smoked bacon, kielbasa, and Bloody Mary sauce to the mix over cheddar-Jack stone-ground grits; Hook & Barrel, which smokes their shrimp with andouille sausage and tricolored peppers in a smoked tomato broth; and Bistro 217, which serves it as a small plate, with bacon, mushrooms, Tabasco, white wine, butter garlic, and tomatoes over a fried grit cake.

Blueberry's Grill
7931 N Kings Hwy., Myrtle Beach, 843-945-4588
4586 Hwy. 17 S, North Myrtle Beach
blueberrysgrill.com

Hook & Barrel
8014 N Kings Hwy., Myrtle Beach, 843-839-5888
hookandbarrelrestaurant.com

Bistro 217
10707 Ocean Hwy., Pawleys Island, 843-235-8217
bistro217.com

11

PUT YOUR HANDS ON A BURGER
AT RIVER CITY CAFE

The always-fresh, never-frozen burgers at River City Cafe have garnered local and national recognition, but you'll have to put your hands on the buns of one of their burgers to believe it for yourself. With seven locations in the Myrtle Beach area, River City is burger royalty in these parts. Take a seat at a table wrapped in brown butcher paper especially for doodling, wonder at all the state-to-state license plates mounted wall-to-ceiling, and then crack open some peanut shells before you toss them on the hardwood floor. There are a whopping 25 burgers to choose from, plus chicken burgers, a turkey burger, and prime rib short burger. Standouts include the peanut butter bacon burger; the fried mac & cheese burger topped with American cheese and a breaded loaf of fried mac & cheese; and the nacho crunch burger topped with Doritos, jalapeños, pepper jack, guacamole, and spicy chipotle mayo.

404 21st Ave. N, Myrtle Beach, 843-448-1990
9550 Shore Dr. (inside Sands Ocean Resort), Myrtle Beach, 843-497-5299
208 73rd Ave. N, Myrtle Beach, 843-449-8877
4742 Hwy. 17 S (inside Barefoot Landing), North Myrtle Beach, 843-272-7077
4393 Hwy. 17, Murrells Inlet, 843-651-1004
11 N Seaside Dr., Surfside Beach, 843-232-9797
5835 Dick Pond Rd., Socastee, 843-215-8808
rivercitycafe.com

MORE GREAT BURGER JOINTS

Burky's Grill
4001 N Kings Hwy., Myrtle Beach, 843-626-2888
facebook.com/burkysgrill

Hamburger Joe's
712 48th Ave. S, North Myrtle Beach, 843-272-6834
hamburgerjoes.com

Island Bar & Grill
2272 Glenns Bay Rd., Surfside Beach, 843-650-3157
facebook.com/islandbarsurfside

Art Burger Sushi Bar
700 N Ocean Blvd., Myrtle Beach, 843-839-4774
artburgerbar.com

Greg's Cabana Bar & Grill
2800 US 17 Business, Murrells Inlet, 843-651-1836
gregscabana.com

12

DISCOVER THE SECRET GARDEN
AT FRANK'S OUTBACK

I first fell in love with Frank's Outback on one of my first dates nine years ago with my now husband. Frank's is also where we held our intimate wedding reception. The alfresco dining space that's "out back" behind Frank's Restaurant & Bar is a Pawleys Island landmark that's nationally renowned and has been around since 1992, but you can't see it from Ocean Highway, which is why I fondly call it a "Secret Garden." After sunset, the partially enclosed courtyard and "way back" dining patio turn magical, with strings of white lights draped throughout the canopy of palmettos and potted ferns, pockets of tables tucked into cozy corners here and there, two bars, and brick fireplaces. And the beautiful thing about Frank's ambiance and coastal-inspired dinner menu is that it's undoubtedly the highest quality, hands down, but not too froufrou or unapproachable.

10434 Ocean Hwy., Pawleys Island, 843-237-3030
franksandoutback.com

13

CONTINUE THE LEGACY
AT MR. SUB

When I used to work at the *Sun News* years ago, many lunch breaks were spent driving just down the road to Mr. Sub in downtown Myrtle Beach next to city hall. It's where many tourists, summer after summer, first stop to pick up lunch when they get to town for vacation. The building has been standing there since 1964, and Ken and Tommy Conley opened Mr. Sub in 1979 after they moved to the beach from Pittsburgh, running it for the next 43 years until March 2022, when they decided to retire. The new owners didn't skip a beat when the closing of the beloved institution left a void in this section of downtown, bringing the building up to code and reopening for business before the summer tourism season on May 1, 2023. Continue the legacy and order the pastrami sub, supersized, with mayo, mustard, lettuce, and tomatoes (I hold the onions).

1011 E Broadway St., Myrtle Beach, 843-232-7833
mr-sub.com

HAVE
A BOWERY BEER

They say "there's never a dull moment" at The Bowery, which is saying a lot for this landmark bar of nearly 80 years serving beer, music, and good times just steps from the boardwalk, the ocean, and the open lawn where the old Pavilion amusement park once stood. The saloon-style, log cabin facade should indicate what awaits behind The Bowery's doors, which is unapologetically beach bar rustic—and you can't help but love it. Order a Bowery Beer (their own "brew") and soak in the history of this place because it also doubles as a museum. It's where country music mega-group Alabama got its start as the house band in the 1970s with hits like "Dancin', Shaggin' on the Boulevard." It's where Price "Scuba" Osborne broke the Guinness World Record for carrying 34 mugs of beer 100 feet without spilling a drop. (He left his job at The Bowery in 1980, when Alabama left the building to go national, to be a crew member.) And it's where you'll make your own memories.

110 9th Ave. N, Myrtle Beach, 843-626-3445
thebowery.com

15

PARK IT
AT THE FOOD TRUCK FESTIVAL

Every year, when the ocean breeze is thawing out the winter cold and signaling that spring is around the corner, the Myrtle Beach Food Truck Festival takes over the large oceanfront lawn bordering the boardwalk that used to be home to the Pavilion. The massive festival in late March/early April showcases more than 50 food trucks cooking up a melting pot of different foods, from burgers and snacks to barbecue, Mexican, hibachi, desserts, coffee, booze pops, and more. If that's not enough, the three-day Food Truck Festival also adds to the fun with artisans selling their handcrafted wares, a lineup of live entertainment, beer and wine vendors, and local businesses, too. It's an all-day affair for the entire family to graze and laze under the Carolina sun overlooking the blue waters of the Atlantic.

Burroughs & Chapin Pavilion Pl., 812 N Ocean Blvd., Myrtle Beach
nspromos.com/mbfoodtruckfest

TIP

The food festival is conveniently located just steps away from the Myrtle Beach Boardwalk, so, after you've had your fill of food and drinks, take the family on a stroll on the pleasant oceanfront boards.

16

BREAK BREAD
AT BENJAMIN'S BAKERY

Benjamin's Bakery, Cafe, and Coffee Roasters has been a well-known name throughout Myrtle Beach's households, grocery stores, and restaurants for their fresh-baked bagels since 1994. Since then, they've expanded into baking an assortment of breads, rolls, pastries, and cakes, plus serving breakfast and lunch sandwiches in the café, and roasting coffee in-house. Their yummy food offerings are scrawled on their blackboard menu. (I like the Poplar Drive sandwich stacked with turkey, provolone, spinach, tomato, and bacon on a grilled baguette with basil pesto mayo with a side of bagel chips and spicy hummus.) It's also the feeling of community that's served here at this corner café daily. Book clubs meet here at the tables or couches, locals linger and catch up, and it's where I often work at my laptop, while founder Lee Zulanch makes his rounds to meet and greet his customers with a smile and a, "Hello, Sunshine!"

810 3rd Ave. S, Surfside Beach, 843-477-1100
benjaminsbakery.com

17

SIP ON A MARGARITA
AT SUN CITY CAFÉ

Famous for their salted mugs of margaritas on the rocks, Sun City Café is also a locals' favorite for creative Mexican dishes they admit are not authentic Mexican but what they call "Myrtle Mex." Open since 2001, this cozy café in downtown Myrtle Beach not only serves up delicious art on a plate but also colorful, quirky surroundings in every square inch of the dining room (think mannequin busts and a disco ball) that will have you spotting something new on each visit. In addition to the must-order margarita, try Sun City's Shrimp Dip laced with chipotle, the slow-braised chicken taco, and any of the burritos smacked with a twist: smashed potatoes. Then, they roll the burrito in their cheese sauce and salsa (prepared fresh daily); bake it in the oven; and top it with lettuce, tomato, and sour cream before it arrives in front of you. Olé!

801 Main St., Myrtle Beach, 843-445-2992
suncitycafemb.com

TIP

Sun City Café is only open for dinner from 5 to 9 p.m. Wednesday through Saturday, so plan ahead!

18

ROCK A SUSHI ROLL
AT ROLLIN LOCAL

Historic Georgetown's Front Street has recently experienced quite a resurgence in its restaurant scene, with Rollin Local among them. It sits on the corner of Front and Broad Streets in the charming former People's Bank building that dates back to 1906. Choose to dine alfresco along Front Street or inside amid the rustic Southern surroundings. And then feast your eyes on Rollin Local's menu that lists an abundance of sushi rolls—35 specialty, 11 classic, and 12 nigiri and sashimi, to be exact—that are rolled, stuffed, and artistically topped with a uniquely creative combo of fresh ingredients. There's the award-winning Sexy Roll with snow crab meat, fried onions, mango, cilantro, shrimp, and jalapeños topped with tuna, black caviar, spicy mayo, and kimchi wasabi sauce; or try the SC Crunch Roll packed with the delicious crunch of tempura crab, jalapeño, and cream cheese, and then topped with avocado, shrimp, eel sauce, and spicy mayo. Finish it off with a bottle of Lucky Buddha beer.

732 Front St., Georgetown, 843-485-4345

MORE SUSHI SPOTS

Wicked Tuna
4123 US 17 Business, Murrells Inlet, 843-651-9987
2nd Ave. Pier, 110 N Ocean Blvd., 843-712-2430
thewickedtuna.com

Wahoo's Fish House
3993 US 17 Business, Murrells Inlet, 843-651-5800
wahoosfishhouse.com

39th Ave. Bar & Grille
3809 Hwy. 17 S, North Myrtle Beach, 843-427-7080
39thavenuebarandgrille.com

Boardwalk Billy's
1407 13th Ave. N, North Myrtle Beach, 843-249-0900
boardwalkbillysnmb.com

19

FIND THE HIDDEN SPEAKEASY
AT TWELVE 33 DISTILLERY

Twelve 33 Distillery is one of 17 distilleries in South Carolina but may be one of the only distilleries with a hidden speakeasy. You'll be able to sit yourself down in a padded brown leather armchair and take in the dark, sexy confines of their speakeasy at the conclusion of the VIP Tour. Husband-wife owners Kevin and Rebecca Osborn have made their mark in the Little River community, converting the bones of a huge beach store into a craft distillery, with wall-to-wall windows, clean woodwork, a sleek window display of all the metal distilling tanks and equipment, and a marriage of modern and rustic elements. The name Twelve 33 is coined from the date that Prohibition ended on December 5, 1933. This distillery produces nine handcrafted spirits from locally sourced grains and fresh ingredients: vodka, gin, rum, and whiskey varietals in small batches.

593 SC-90 E, Little River, 843-663-3344
twelve33distillery.com

TIP

Stop by to sample from Twelve 33's tasting menu, order from any of the dozen seasonal signature cocktails, or take a guided tour.

20

TRY EINKORN PASTA
AT INDULGE ITALIAN EATERY

What is einkorn? For more than 12,000 years, the ancient einkorn wheat grain has been planted and eaten by humans, but it's only recently been on the food industry's radar, including Indulge Italian Eatery here in Carolina Forest, one of only a handful of restaurants on the East Coast serving it on their menu. The difference in einkorn, compared to other grains, is that it has not been genetically modified or changed by humans, which means it has the same amount of gluten as modern farmed wheat, but its proteins are smaller and easier to digest, actually scoring a zero on the Gluten Index and performing gentler on digestion. And that's a blessing for those with gluten allergies, who can now safely digest the handcrafted einkorn pasta dishes at Indulge. Try the chicken piccata, served with einkorn fettucine pasta in a caper lemon sauce that is melt-in-your-mouth amazing.

4999 Carolina Forest Blvd., Myrtle Beach, 843-903-7946
indulgeitalianeatery.com

21

SIT ON A CORNER
AT PEACHES OR SAM'S

There are two legendary corner cafés in the Myrtle Beach area—Peaches Corner and Sam's Corner—that you just have to experience for the nostalgia of it all. Peaches, at the corner of Ninth Avenue North and Ocean Boulevard in the heart of the city of Myrtle Beach, has been around the block since 1937. The only one left in the Carolinas, Peaches is named after the original owner's name, Peach Justice, or "Momma Peach," and the restaurant is still in the family today. Order their world-famous Peaches Burger or footlong hot dog smothered with slaw, mustard, chili, and onions. The family-owned Sam's Corner at the corner of Atlantic Avenue and Waccamaw Drive in Garden City is also a time machine, with the same booths and metal signs in place since opening 47 years ago. Sam's is open 24 hours, so you can grab eggs, biscuits, and grits for breakfast and their award-winning pimento cheeseburger, hot dogs, fries, and more for lunch and dinner.

Peaches Corner
900 N Ocean Blvd., Myrtle Beach, 843-448-7424
peachescorner.com

Sam's Corner
101 Atlantic Ave., Garden City, 843-651-3233
facebook.com/samscornergc

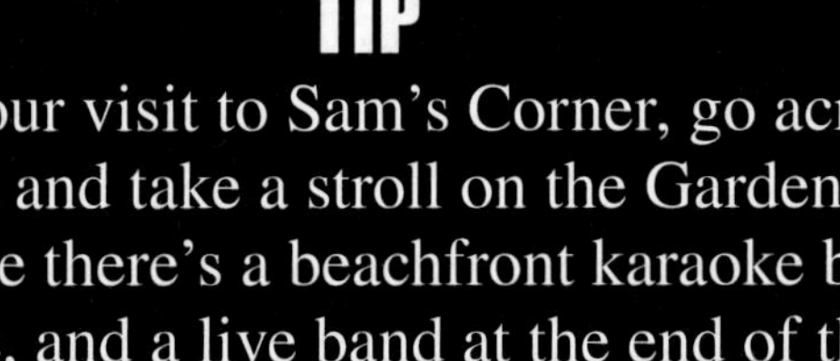

TIP

After your visit to Sam's Corner, go across the street and take a stroll on the Garden City Pier, where there's a beachfront karaoke bar, an arcade, and a live band at the end of the pier during the summer.

22

DIG THROUGH BARBECUE
AT BUBBA'S

Bubba's Fish Camp and Smokehouse on the outskirts of Broadway at the Beach looks like a giant, upscale bait and tackle shop, wrapped in corrugated metal panels and industrial garage doors to let the beach breeze in. True to its name, inside, the heady scent of smoked meats slow-cooking for hours wafts from the 750-pound Cookshack Fast Eddy's smoker that the chef and back of the house nicknamed "Sally." A good way to sample just about everything on the smokehouse's menu is to order "The PIT Boss," a heaping platter of pulled pork, pork sausage, quarter chicken, and baby back pork ribs, plus sides of crinkle french fries, coleslaw, hush puppies, and brown baked beans. All the meats are tender, juicy, and packed with flavor. Add more by drizzling your choice of mustard- or vinegar-based sauces. Bubba's smoked meats are dry brined with house seasonings and then smoked low and slow in the smoker every day.

1565 21st Ave. N, Myrtle Beach, 843-839-0505
bubbasfishcamp.com

MORE GREAT BARBECUE PLACES

Simply Southern Smokehouse
1913 Mr. Joe White Ave., Myrtle Beach, 843-839-1913
simplysouthernsmokehouse.com

Little Pigs Bar-B-Q
6102 Frontage Rd., Myrtle Beach, 843-692-9774
littlepigsmyrtlebeach.com

Gracious Pig Smokehouse
12 Ocean Blvd., Surfside Beach, 843-945-2017
graciouspig.com

Back Home BBQ
3750 US 17 Business, Murrells Inlet, 843-357-1133
backhomebbq.net

Hog Heaven
7147 Ocean Hwy., Pawleys Island, 843-237-7444
hogheaveninc.com

23

SHAKE THINGS UP
AT THE CRAZY MASON

It's a milkshake. It's a milkshake/ice cream dessert on steroids. And it's what's on the menu at The Crazy Mason. Just like their sweet ingredients overflow from the top of the mason jars, this popular milkshake bar has expanded by demand into other markets in the Southeast, but the original one was right here in Myrtle Beach. The Mason uses more than 100 ingredients, as well as locally grown produce and treats from local bakeries, and just stacks them into over-the-top, Insta pic-worthy shakes and desserts. The challenge will just be deciding on which one of the many Crazy Masons to dig into. The Don't Worry Beach Happy combo is a good one: orange swirl ice cream stuffed into a mason jar rimmed with vanilla buttercream icing rolled in crushed graham crackers, and then topped with a wave of cotton candy, a custom beach sugar cookie, whipped cream, and more crushed graham crackers.

2461 Coastal Grand Cir., Myrtle Beach
thecrazymason.com

HEAT THINGS UP
AT BLUE ELEPHANT THAI CUISINE

The Blue Elephant is at the end of a basic, inconspicuous blue building south of the MarshWalk in Murrells Inlet, but, trust me, you will love the food, the ambiance, and the experience of this authentic Thai restaurant. Spot the royal-blue elephant sign with trunk pointed skyward (an expression to greet visitors with happiness), step foot inside, sit down, and enjoy a trip to Thailand. All dishes are prepared and made to order with fresh ingredients and spices imported from China by executive chef Dr. Paul Byington, and the time is worth it. The intimate dining room is ornate, with tables dressed in white linen cloths and entrées artfully plated on exquisite china. Start with the tom kha gai (coconut chicken soup), and then explore the four different curries in house entrées, specialties and seafood dishes, and noodle creations prepared in a scale of spicy heat from mild to authentic. (Beware!)

4493 US-17 Business, Murrells Inlet, 843-651-5863

TIP

Seating at Blue Elephant is intimate, so keep in mind that reservations fill up fast!

25

HELP CHEFS IN TRAINING
AT THE INTERNATIONAL CULINARY INSTITUTE OF MYRTLE BEACH

You will be amazed at the student-operated Fowler Dining Room in the International Culinary Institute (ICI) on the Grand Strand Campus of Horry Georgetown Technical College. This isn't your typical school cafeteria; it's true chef training in a classroom that doubles as an actual fine dining restaurant with sleek, modern surroundings. Book lunch for $25 and be wowed by the fruits of the labor from this student talent that range in cooking techniques, with a focus on taste, texture, color, and creativity using locally grown vegetables, fruits, meats, seafood, cheese, and eggs. Menus rotate weekly and travel to a different part of the country or globe. Past menu themes were "Florida and the Nuevo Latino Food Movement," featuring flavors from Latin America and the Caribbean, and "Southern Louisiana's Soul Food," which explored the impact of Cajun and Creole cuisines on traditional Southern foods.

920 Crabtree Ln., Myrtle Beach, 843-839-7001
hgtc.edu/academics/academic-departments/culinary-institute

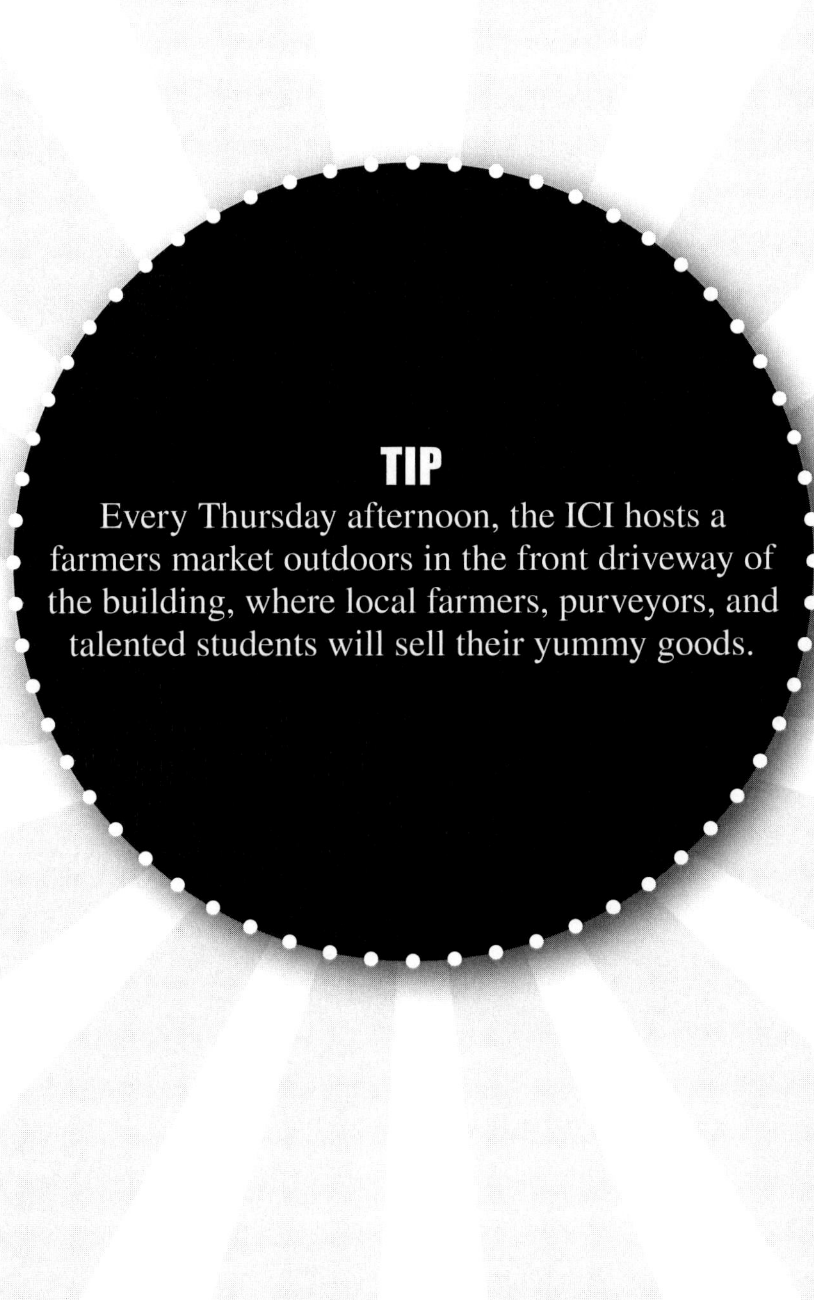

TIP

Every Thursday afternoon, the ICI hosts a farmers market outdoors in the front driveway of the building, where local farmers, purveyors, and talented students will sell their yummy goods.

26

SIP ON MUSCADINE WINE
AT LA BELLE AMIE VINEYARD

Tucked away in a forest surrounding an old family farm boasting vines more than 150 years old, La Belle Amie Vineyard features a tasting room and outdoor deck that was built in 1999 and today offers a line of muscadine wines, a full schedule of live music and festivals on the property, and a retail shop with regular tastings. No matter how you choose to experience La Belle Amie, you'll love the revelry that is contagious at the vineyard. Their Twisted Sisters line includes reds, whites, and rosés pressed from the muscadine grapes native to our sandy soil here at the beach for a much sweeter finish. Sip on the Bless Her Heart drier white, Cabana Boy peachy white, Ice Queen sweet, sweet white, or Sweet Baby Blues blueberry blend—or all four!

1120 St. Joseph Rd., Little River, 843-399-9463
labelleamie.com

27

ENJOY THE SEAFOOD SALAD WITH SOME SEA BREEZE

AT CONCH CAFE

Serving up good vibes since 1984, Conch Cafe is a charming, beachfront bungalow where you can eat fresh seafood on the raised, covered porch while you look out at the ocean and feel her sweet sea breeze wash over you. I've never actually dined inside—only outdoors on the beachfront back porch, where pets are also allowed to join you. From the light fare section of the menu, I recommend for lunch their salad platter, a sampling of four of their homemade salads: tuna, chicken, seafood, and shrimp and pasta. They're all fresh, light, and delicious. Add to your order an ice-cold cocktail. And, after you've paid your check, walk down the stairs to the sand, kick off your flip-flops, and take a walk barefoot down the beach or enjoy a post-lunch workout.

1870 N Waccamaw Dr., Garden City, 843-651-6556
conchcafe.net

28

TAKE IN THE SUNSET
AT GULFSTREAM CAFE

Gulfstream Cafe is one of the best spots on the coastline to watch the sun slip into the horizon for a picturesque sunset show from their rooftop deck. Since 1984, the waterfront Gulfstream has stood near the end of the point where the inlet marsh meets the ocean next door to Marlin Quay Marina, and it seems that the sky wraps around you in a panoramic lens embrace. The laid-back, long-standing restaurant has been known as a meeting spot for special family celebrations, date nights, or Sunday brunch with a menu of coastal cuisine, fresh seafood, and Southern classics. Try the Sunset Tower, a platter for the whole table of a half pound of shrimp, a half dozen oysters, and lobster tails served with cocktail sauce and butter or the jumbo lump crab cakes with mustard sauce, mashed potatoes, and seasonal veggies.

1536 S Waccamaw Dr., Garden City, 843-651-8808
gulfstreamcafe.com

GIVE THANKS
AT THE PARSON'S TABLE

Dating back to 1885, the first Little River Methodist Church was resurrected into the main dining room of Parson's Table. And you will sing all the praises of today's Parson's Table, like the sawed logs for the church still standing as the original wood of the restaurant and clapboard pine walls inside, the hardwood flooring sourced from a farmhouse built in the 1850s, the large chandelier and stained glass windows that once hung in a Baptist church in Mullins, and the large, antique front doors crafted from local cypress that are over 150 years old. There is local history at every turn of this beloved institution, but also a locally sourced philosophy working with local farmers, fishermen, and vendors to create a coastal Carolina menu that will have you bowing down to the chef.

4305 McCorsley Ave., Little River, 843-249-3702
parsonstable.com

30

EAT UP THE NOSTALGIA
AT HOSKINS RESTAURANT

Hoskins Restaurant is still one of the few mom-and-pop restaurants on Main Street in North Myrtle Beach, going strong since 1948. Family-owned, Hoskins has changed hands over the years, from Hubert and Leona Hoskins, to Leona's daughter and son-in-law after Hubert's untimely death in 1955, and then to a string of other family member owners since then. Serving breakfast, lunch, and dinner, Hoskins is known for their fried seafood, fried chicken, steaks, and pork chops served with sides like homemade coleslaw, hush puppies, sweet potato fries, and more. Lunch specials change up daily, so expect to see a line of people out the door waiting to be seated inside Hoskins during the summer. You may even spot celebrity Vanna White, who likes to drop by at her hometown favorite restaurant when she's back here for a visit!

405 Main St., North Myrtle Beach, 843-249-2014
hoskinsrestaurant.com

FEED SOMEONE IN NEED
AT WINNA'S KITCHEN

Winna's Kitchen in downtown Myrtle Beach is a delicious culinary and community experience. Open Wednesday through Saturday for lunch and brunch, Winna's menu features its anchor section and one that rotates seasonally to reflect local ingredients that are available. Try one of their toasts; the Ricardo Toast is thick-sliced, country white bread toasted and finished with sweetened ricotta, grilled fruit, balsamic, honey, and pistachios. The seasonal chicken salad is also a must: either their sweet and smoky hatch chile bacon or a light and zesty lemon basil blend. If you order a "No. 1" for $5 on your visit, Winna's will provide a meal for a person in need. A special treat is the Winna's at Night dinner tasting menu, featuring up to seven courses of global cuisine on select Friday or Saturday evenings that requires reservations.

819 Main St., Myrtle Beach, 843-945-8181
winnaskitchen.com

Family Kingdom

MUSIC AND ENTERTAINMENT

ANCHOR FOR A LIVE CONCERT AT THE BOATHOUSE

The sounds of summer are echoed along the Intracoastal Waterway from the Landing at The Boathouse, which hosts a live summer concert series from their waterfront stage on the banks of the river. A true Sunday fun day, this free concert series has been a tradition every Sunday at 5 p.m. from April through the first week of September since 2008. The Boathouse has welcomed nationally known rock, country, reggae, hip-hop, and tribute bands onto their stage. Concertgoers either congregate on blankets and lawn chairs on the Boathouse's backyard or they come by boat in droves and anchor together in the water on the backside of the stage. Picnic tables, bar tops, cornhole boards, and more fun are also scattered at the adjoining Independent Republic Brewing Company microbrewery and beer garden, plus a plethora of food options.

201 Fantasy Harbour Blvd., Myrtle Beach, 843-903-2628
landingmb.com

HEAR THE MUSIC
AT HOUSE OF BLUES

Although House of Blues concert venues are dotted across the country, our House of Blues Myrtle Beach location in Barefoot Landing is still a vital source of music and entertainment for our locals craving live music. There are a handful of ways to satisfy those cravings at the House: live concerts (requiring tickets) on the main stage from national touring acts, free live music on the back deck off the restaurant bar in the warmer months, the weekly Murder Mystery Dinner featuring interactive comedy and a three-course meal, and the Sunday Gospel Brunch, complete with a buffet of Southern-inspired goodness and live gospel music to inspire. Grab a table to get a bite before the show of your choice and you will not be disappointed. I like their BBQ nachos or loaded fries with jalapeño-bacon, pickled red onion, cheddar cheese, cilantro crema, and cotija cheese.

4640 Hwy. 17 S, North Myrtle Beach, 843-272-3000
houseofblues.com/myrtlebeach

34

TAKE A SEAT
AT THE ALABAMA THEATRE

Once again, country music stars Alabama have left their imprint on Myrtle Beach, where they first rose to fame at The Bowery, with their desire to kick-start the entertainment industry in our area through the birth of the Alabama Theatre. This iconic theater in Barefoot Landing has been entertaining locals and tourists since 1993. Always reinventing themselves, Alabama Theatre updated their once famous *ONE The Show* to *Iconic*, which showcases new choreography and song selections, plus more comedy, thrills, and riveting entertainment. When the holidays reign at the beach, Alabama Theatre performs their *South's Grandest Christmas Show* to get the entire family in the joyful Christmas spirit. And the rest of the theater's entertainment calendar is filled with performances by some of the country's biggest artists in country, Motown, pop, and comedy.

4750 Hwy. 17 S, North Myrtle Beach, 843-272-1111
alabama-theatre.com

RIDE SKY-HIGH
ON THE SKYWHEEL

SkyWheel Myrtle Beach is the first thing you spy with your little eye in our skyline, night or day, and it was one of the first observation wheels of its kind in the United States when it took its first spin in 2011. Fly to new heights to get a bird's-eye view of the coastline from 200 feet above ground and within one of the 42 cool, climate-controlled gondolas. Just sit back and relax! SkyWheel Myrtle Beach welcomes riders of all ages and offers special VIP, engagement, and gender reveal packages. And when your feet are back on the ground, browse the souvenirs at the gift shop to remember your flight and grab some grub and cold drinks at LandShark Bar & Grill, just steps away from the SkyWheel.

1110 N Ocean Blvd., Myrtle Beach, 843-839-9200
skywheelmb.com

CLAP ALONG
AT THE CAROLINA OPRY

Nashville may have the Grand Ole Opry, but Myrtle Beach has the Carolina Opry Theater. With founder Calvin Gilmore at the helm, the stage curtains first rose at The Carolina Opry in 1986, and the theater has been producing a rotation of award-winning shows ever since. The three main productions that hit the stage regularly are *The Carolina Opry*, a variety show of live music, comedy, and dance, including the fan-favorite, hip-hop cloggers All That! of *America's Got Talent*; *Time Warp*, a live music tribute to the best music of the '60s, '70s, and '80s; and *The Christmas Show of the South*, featuring more than 35 of the nation's most talented artists, a real horse-drawn sleigh, stunning costuming, and special effects. The Opry also hosts a calendar full of live concerts performed by some of the best tribute bands in the country.

8901 N Kings Hwy., Myrtle Beach, 843-913-4000
thecarolinaopry.com

37

BOOT SCOOT
AT THE CAROLINA COUNTRY MUSIC FEST

One of the East Coast's biggest country music festivals, the Carolina Country Music Fest (CCMF) brings tens of thousands who descend on the former oceanfront Pavilion grounds in Myrtle Beach to boot scoot and boogie to a lineup of more than 40 of country music's hottest artists. Since 2015, CCMF brings big-time country names to the beach for four days in early June. Think Kenny Chesney, Miranda Lambert, Brooks & Dunn, Travis Tritt, Tracy Lawrence, Lainey Wilson, Keith Urban, Carrie Underwood, and many more that change up every summer. CCMF spreads love, fun, sun, and country music over the 18-acre festival site bordering the Myrtle Beach Boardwalk. Each day features a full day of national and up-and-coming artists to watch, food and drink vendors, dress-up themes for all concertgoers, and fun selfie backdrops to capture all the memories.

812 N Ocean Blvd., Myrtle Beach
carolinacountrymusicfest.com

TIP

Take your CCMF concert experience to the next level with the four-day Main Stage VIP pass, which gives you access to a private area right in front of the stage, private bathrooms, a VIP cash bar, and free activities. (These sell out fast!)

38

SHARE LAUGHS
AT FAMILY KINGDOM

Family Kingdom Amusement Park has been a family-friendly mainstay in the heart of Myrtle Beach for more than 40 years. Located just across the street from the ocean, the fun-filled park is laid out with more than 35 rides that are updated or rotated out just about every year, ranging from thrill to family, kiddie, and go-kart rides for everyone from the young to the young at heart. Buckle up and ride the OG Swamp Fox Roller Coaster, a wooden coaster that has been a landmark since the park opened in 1966—and you can certainly feel the age as you bump along the 2,400 feet of the all-wooden track as it climbs to the pinnacle for a one-of-a-kind ocean view. Other highlights for all ages are the Twist 'n Shout coaster, log flume, Figure-8 Track, carousel, and Pistolero Round-Up.

300 S Ocean Blvd., Myrtle Beach, 843-626-3447
familykingdomfun.com

WALK LIKE A PIRATE
AT PIRATES VOYAGE

Arrrrgh, mateys, are you ready to come aboard to experience some high-intensity, high-flying action? If not, you may walk the plank at Pirates Voyage, home of an indoor hideaway lagoon arena built around two full-sized pirate ships that are led by Blackbeard and Calico Jack. Your family will love the adventurous performances by mermaids, divers, acrobats, aerialists, tropical birds, sea lions, and daring pirates both high above and diving into the sea below, all unfolding while you dine on a delicious four-course feast—with your hands! The dinner show's dramatic plotline soaked in adventure changes over the holiday season. Be sure to take the kiddos to the preshow, when the excitement builds and they can get transformed into a pirate, complete with hats, an eye patch, and face paint. It's an engaging show that you'll be wowed by from start to cannon finish.

8907 N Kings Hwy., Myrtle Beach, 843-497-9700
piratesvoyage.com/myrtle-beach

40

SHOP, EAT, AND DRINK
AT BROADWAY AT THE BEACH

There's always something happening at Broadway at the Beach, a 350-acre hub of entertainment options that are offered in all shapes and forms encircling Lake Broadway. Since 1995, Broadway, laid out in different villages, has evolved over the years to keep up with the latest trends in all things fun. Unique boutiques abound, and then there are a colorful variety of bars, big-name restaurants (Margaritaville, Hard Rock Cafe, and Dave & Buster's), and nightclubs; WonderWorks; escape rooms and mazes; an aquarium; amusement parks; magic and aerialist theaters; jet boat rides on the lake; zip lines; and much more. You could easily spend a whole day—and be sure to stay for the fireworks show that lights up the sky over the lake on select evenings at 10 p.m. year-round. Beware: parking is a high commodity in the summertime!

1325 Celebrity Cir., Myrtle Beach, 843-444-3200
broadwayatthebeach.com

STROLL AROUND
BAREFOOT LANDING

Similar to Broadway at the Beach, Barefoot Landing is a dining, shopping, and entertainment complex in North Myrtle Beach that surrounds a massive lake and borders the Intracoastal Waterway. You will get a kick out of walking around Barefoot (but I don't recommend doing it barefoot). If you're visiting with your family, I highly suggest Lucy Buffett's (Jimmy Buffett's sister) LuLu's on the waterway, a cool combo of food, drinks, music, and kids' entertainment via the beach play area, ropes course, and arcade. For a party of two, Greg Norman Australian Grille is just for you, with sexy surrounds and cozy alfresco dining waterfront by firepits, wood-grilled steaks, and an award-winning wine list. Then stroll around to discover a cute amusement area complete with a carousel, live music on the Pepsi Stage in the Dockside Village, and a fireworks finale.

4898 Hwy. 17 S, North Myrtle Beach, 843-272-8349
bflanding.com

42

COUNT DOWN NEW YEAR'S EVE AT THE MARKET COMMON

No, it's not Times Square in New York City, but a Southern Times Square New Year's Celebration at The Market Common is just as special here south of the Mason–Dixon. The streets of The Market Common shut down from 9 p.m. to midnight on New Year's Eve and are flooded with lively locals looking to count down to the new year. Also on the big night's agenda is live music on the main stage; vendors selling beer, wine, and bubbly; food vendors offering everything from funnel cakes and sweets to chili dogs and more; a stand with party hats, noisemakers, and glow sticks; kids' activities (face painting, bounce houses, and balloon artist); and a laser light show and ball drop at midnight to ring in a Happy New Year!

4017 Deville St., Myrtle Beach, 843-839-3500
marketcommonmb.com

WALK UNDER A TANK OF SHARKS

AT RIPLEY'S AQUARIUM

Otherwise known as Dangerous Reef (never mind the name), this huge, popular centerpiece aquarium at Ripley's Aquarium will have you walking in a tunnel along the moving, 340-foot-long glidepath open-mouthed, staring up at thousands of fish swimming overhead. Sand tiger sharks, sandbar sharks, nurse sharks, green moray eels, tarpons, green sea turtles, sawfish, giant stingrays, and more thrive here! But there's so much more marine life to come face-to-face with on the two levels of the aquarium. Be wowed by the schools of colorful tropical fish swimming around the reef in Rainbow Rock, lay belly-down on the rocks to feed the rays in Stingray Bay, chill out with the penguins in the Penguin Playhouse, and stare at the mesmerizing live art gallery of jellies in Planet Jellies. The entire family will love it here!

1110 Celebrity Cir., Myrtle Beach, 843-916-0888
ripleyaquariums.com/myrtlebeach

TIP

If you want to take it to the next level, sign up for a sleepover at the aquarium or book a short sail on their glass-bottom boat atop the Dangerous Reef.

44

DANCE ON THE SAND
AT OCEAN ANNIE'S BEACH BAR

Ocean Annie's Beach Bar has been getting rowdy for nearly four decades at the Sands Ocean Club on the north end of Myrtle Beach. Known to kick things up a notch, Ocean Annie's is a hot outdoor bar to cool off with a frozen drink, listen and dance to live music on the pool deck, and let your hair down. That said, it's unapologetically brazen, complete with bikini-clad servers, and, thus, not a place to take the kiddos. While Ocean Annie's is located at a resort, it's open to the public, so take advantage of the good times in the great outdoors with the ocean breeze. Party it up with one of their signature cocktails, like Annie's Tea (vodka, tequila, rum, gin with sour, triple sec, lime, and cola) or the Myrtle Beach Sunset (tequila, triple sec, lime, sour, blue curacao, and lemon-lime soda).

9550 Shore Dr., Myrtle Beach, 888-266-4375
oceananniesresorts.com/ocean-annies

45

GO WILD
AT ALLIGATOR ADVENTURE

Alligators and crocodiles and snakes—oh my! If you're up for a day of all living things creepy and crawly, feathery and wild, head to Alligator Adventure at Barefoot Landing. Dubbed "The Reptile Capital of the World," the park allows your family to meander and explore the wildlife areas, ponds, frog and lizard house, and other exhibits. Besides the variety of alligator species, discover bobcats, flamingos, owls, ostriches, snakes, rams, mountain lions, spotted hyenas, tortoises, and more. And get more up close and personal (if you dare) at their seasonal live shows. These alligator live feedings feature 15-foot alligators leaping out of the water by the command of staff vet Dr. Sam Seashole (or "The Croc Doc"), an alligator-handling show, and snake handling that will teach you some facts about the myths of these reptiles.

4604 Hwy. 17 S, North Myrtle Beach, 843-361-0789
alligatoradventure.com

LEARN HOW TO SHAG
AT FAT HAROLD'S

Get your mind out of the gutter! "Shag," in this case, refers to shag dancing, a hybrid of swing and South Carolina's state dance, which first debuted on the boulevard dance floors of Myrtle Beach in the 1930s and is still alive and well today. Held every March, the National Shag Dance Championships started in Myrtle Beach in 1984 and is the longest continuously running shag dance contest in the country. But, if you're a shag beginner, you can learn the footwork at some local clubs, like the 40-year mainstay Fat Harold's on Main Street in North Myrtle Beach. Lean into the DJ's playlist of beach music and learn the shag moves with free lessons from the pros most Monday and Tuesday nights. Or, if you'd rather be a wallflower, come by on the weekends and watch the dance floor fill with local shaggers.

212 Main St., North Myrtle Beach, 843-249-5779
fatharolds.com

TIP

Twice a year in April and September, the Society of Stranders (SOS) shuts down the streets of North Myrtle Beach with a huge celebration of shag dance parties, workshops, and more events.

MUSIC HOP
ON THE MARSHWALK

The minute your flip-flops hit the half mile of wooden boards that make up the Murrells Inlet MarshWalk on any given night, you'll more than likely hear the sounds of sweet music floating in the air along the water. Where legend says that Blackbeard and other swashbuckling pirates once stashed their booty and guzzled their rum today is widely known for an impressive lineup of seafood restaurants and bars that double as live music venues. Music hop with a drink in hand to groove to everything from beach music to acoustic to country to rock to oldies and more from Bovine's to Drunken Jack's to Wahoo's Fish House to Dead Dog Saloon to Creek Ratz to The Claw House to Wicked Tuna. If that's not enough, the MarshWalk also goes all in to host special annual events, such as a Halloween costume contest, the Santa Crawl, and The Luck of the MarshWalk for St. Patty's.

4025 Hwy. 17 Business, Murrells Inlet
marshwalk.com

ESCAPE
TO THE SURFSIDE BEACH HULA AND FIRE SHOW

You will not want to miss this performance that transports you to the Polynesian islands right here on the sands of Surfside Beach. Every Monday evening throughout the summer, the family business of Ohana Kahakai presents their unforgettable Hula and Fire Show beachfront on the Third Avenue North Beach Access. Ohana, a term meaning “family” in Hawaiian, describes how it was possible for Polynesian voyagers to safely travel thousands of miles to unknown lands on double-hulled canoes by being in touch with nature and the gods. This family, too, brings this Polynesian history and culture to the mainland through this journey one island at a time in the family-friendly show. After the hour showtime, you will have traveled to Hawaii, New Zealand, Tahiti, and Samoa by witnessing the beautiful art of hula dance and fire knife.

3rd Ave. North Beach Access, Surfside Beach
facebook.com/ohanakahakai

TIP

Street parking fills up fast, as does the crowd that gathers on the beach, so bring your beach chairs and set up early!

LISTEN TO THE SOUNDS
OF THE LONG BAY SYMPHONY

Myrtle Beach's music scene isn't just about honky-tonk country or beach music. We actually have our own professional symphony, too. Founded in 1984, The Long Bay Symphony (LBS) is an orchestra comprised of more than 70 members, each boasting quite an accomplished repertoire on a wide range of instruments. Led by conductor Charles Evans Jones, LBS treats local audiences to a season of classical favorites by well-known composers as part of their Masterworks Series; as well as Pop Series concerts that feature fan-favorite popular music from the likes of Queen, ABBA, and more; and special musical events that partner with local charities, like their long-running Bravo Broadway concert. All concerts are held at the Myrtle Beach High School Music and Arts Center. LBS also hosts youth orchestra showcases, galas, fundraisers, and community outreach events throughout the year.

1107 48th Ave. N, Myrtle Beach, 843-448-8379
longbaysymphony.com

GET A BUTTERFLY KISS
AT THE LOWCOUNTRY ZOO

Tucked within Brookgreen Gardens, the Lowcountry Zoo is definitely worth exploring with your admission to Brookgreen. The zoo is one of five organizations in South Carolina that are accredited by the Association of Zoos and Aquariums and tends to house native animals that were either bred and raised in captivity in other zoos or have a major disability because of an injury and wouldn't survive in the wild. Expect to see alligators, bald eagles, gray and red foxes, hawks, owls, the cutest river otters, white-tailed deer, herons, and the endangered red wolves in a new exhibit. Also, a must-see at the zoo is the seasonal Whispering Wings Butterfly Exhibit, where you enter an enclosed garden teeming with tropical plants and hundreds of wild butterflies fluttering in the air that could perch on your shoulders.

1931 Brookgreen Garden Dr., Murrells Inlet, 843-235-6000
brookgreen.org/low-country-zoo

TIP

Your entry to Brookgreen Gardens covers your admission to the Lowcountry Zoo, too, for a full day of exploring all the other lovely things that live in the garden!

TRY YOUR LUCK
AT THE BIG M CASINO

While gambling is illegal in the state of South Carolina, Myrtle Beach has found a way around having a casino's doors open on land. The Big M Casino luxury mega yacht travels out to sea at least three miles and as far as 15 miles to reach international waters (about 45 minutes away) where gambling is allowed. It's the only casino in the state! After the 45-minute mark, you can take a seat at your favorite slot machines and play away, like Pot O'Gold, Wheel of Fortune, or video poker. Or slide over to a table game of blackjack, Let It Ride, three-card poker, craps, or roulette. During the five-hour tour, order wraps, sandwiches, soups, salads, pizzas, and more, plus drinks from the bar. The Big M Casino reportedly pays out an average of $383,000 a week!

4491 Mineola Ave., Little River, 843-249-9811
bigmcasino.com

SPORTS AND RECREATION

WAVE AN AMERICAN FLAG AT THE MURRELLS INLET FOURTH OF JULY BOAT PARADE

Everybody loves a parade—and the Murrells Inlet Boat Parade on the Fourth of July is no exception! A patriotic tradition that's more than 40 years strong, the boat parade sets off from the Garden City Point and slowly winds through the channel along the Murrells Inlet MarshWalk south to Hot Fish Club. The parade's start time varies each year, depending on when high tide falls, and boat owners (and passengers) go all out on the annually rotating boat decorating themes, with the latest being "Made in the USA." Spectators pack every square inch of the MarshWalk on the parade's route, including the main viewing areas south of that at Belin United Methodist Church and Morse Park Landing. Expect to get sprayed by water guns, hoses, and cannons that boaters are armed with onboard! The grand finale for the holiday? Fireworks after sunset over the marsh.

Waterfront, Murrells Inlet, 843-652-4236
facebook.com/murrellsinletboatparade

WAKEBOARD
AT SHARK WAKE PARK

If you have always wanted to learn how to wakeboard, but you don't own a boat to pull one, hit the cables and water at the state-of-the-art Shark Wake Park. No matter your skill level, you can learn to wakeboard, kneeboard, water-ski, wakeskate, or foilboard around the lake by a high-tech pulley system that picks up ropes from the starting dock and pulls riders in a circle. Beginners can take it slow, or seasoned pros can jump the ramps and rails on the sides to try some new tricks. If you'd rather slip, slide, and climb, check out Obstacle Island floating on the adjoining lake. The massive floating playground of adventures features monkey bars, swing ropes, towers to climb, slides, and more for all ages.

150 Citizens Cir., Little River, 843-399-9253
sharkwakepark.com

TIP

After you've worked up an appetite on the water, take a seat at the shaded outdoor Shark Shack, where they serve beer, wine, snacks, cold beverages, ice cream and Pumphouse cold brew coffee on tap. Or, if you're bowing out of the boards, sit back at the Shack and enjoy the 360-degree views of the park while the others ride.

HIKE, BIKE, AND FISH
AT THE STATE PARKS

Our Myrtle Beach coastline boasts two state parks—Myrtle Beach State Park and Huntington Beach State Park—where the great outdoors beckon and offer a varied landscape of sports and rec options. Myrtle Beach State Park, the oldest state park in the state, features a couple of hiking trails on easy terrain; biking on the park's paved roadways or hard, flat beach at low tide on the offseason; and a great, long pier for fishing and crabbing. Huntington Beach State Park, which is widely known for the bird-watchers who flock to the main causeway, also features two hiking trails through the maritime forest, as well as the super-fun, paved Waccamaw Neck Bikeway that parallels US 17 from north of the park in Murrells Inlet and stretches south to Pawleys Island. Huntington also draws local fishermen to the jetties that border the park for prime surf fishing.

Myrtle Beach State Park
4401 S Kings Hwy., Myrtle Beach, 843-238-5325
southcarolinaparks.com/myrtle-beach

Huntington Beach State Park
16148 Ocean Hwy., Murrells Inlet, 843-237-4440
southcarolinaparks.com/huntington-beach

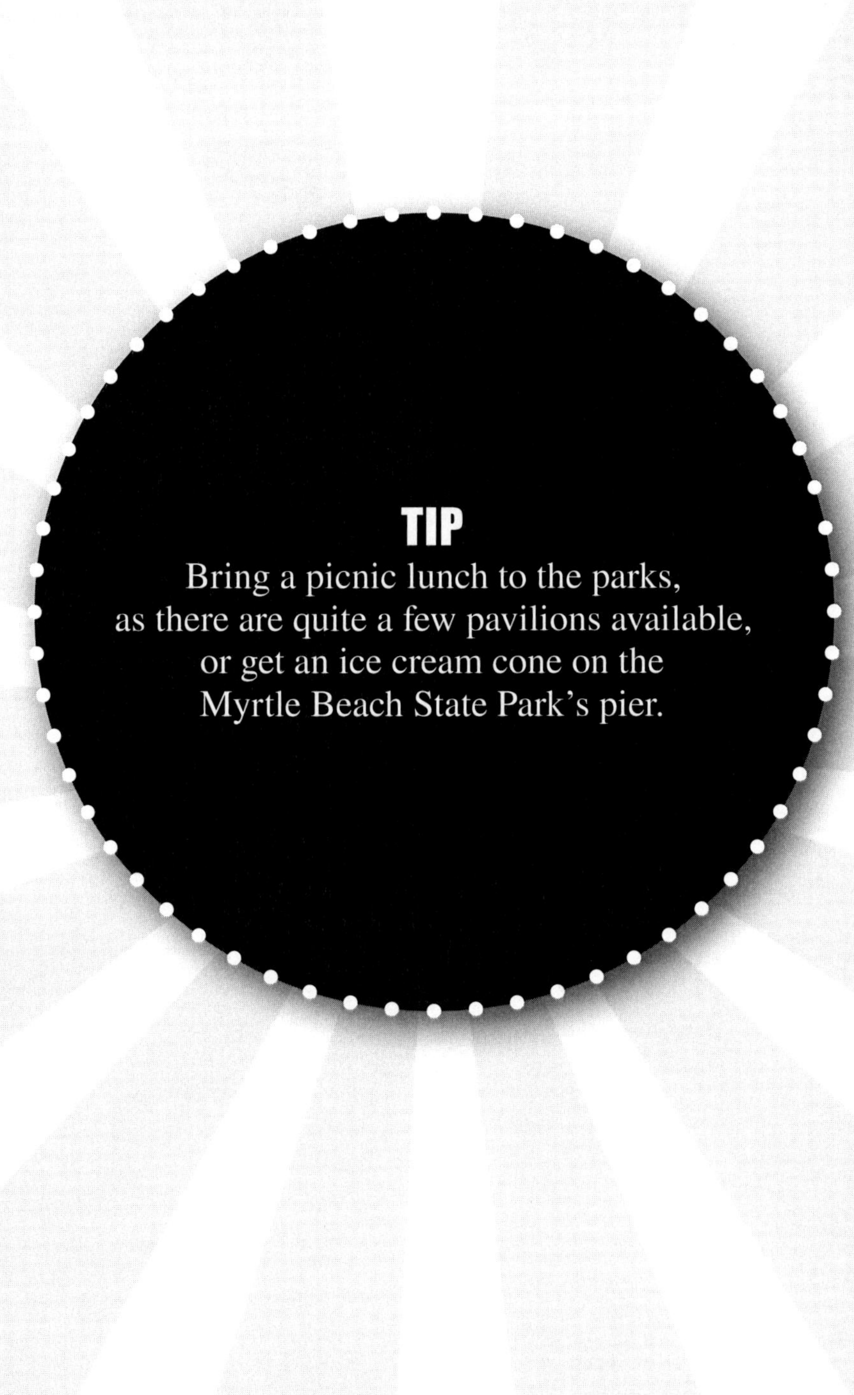
TIP
Bring a picnic lunch to the parks,
as there are quite a few pavilions available,
or get an ice cream cone on the
Myrtle Beach State Park's pier.

SINK YOUR TOES IN THE SAND
AT PELICANS BALLPARK

Our hometown minor-league baseball team, the Myrtle Beach Pelicans, is a Single-A affiliate team of the Chicago Cubs competing in the Carolina League. Pelicans Ballpark has welcomed fans since 1999 and kept up with the trends to keep them coming over the years. The two-level stadium that catches the ocean breeze in center field features luxury suite skyboxes, a kids' inflatable area, grill and picnic area, and Tito's Beach Party on the third base line complete with beach chairs and sand on the ground. Besides nine innings of baseball, there's fun entertainment between innings: weekly promotions, like $2 Budweiser Thirsty Thursdays; an appearance on the bases by Slider, the Pelicans' specially trained bat dog; and food offerings beyond a hot dog and a Coke, like crab cakes, burgers, pulled pork sandwiches, fried pickle chips, waffle ice cream treats, craft beer, and wine.

1251 21st Ave. N, Myrtle Beach, 843-918-6000
milb.com/myrtle-beach

If you come to game day on a Friday, you're in for a special treat: there is a postgame Fireworks Extravaganza, a family meal deal, kid-friendly themes, and kids 12 and under can actually run the bases after the fireworks show.

TAKE A KAYAK TOUR
TO WATIES ISLAND

Waties Island, an undeveloped barrier island to the north of Myrtle Beach, is a slice of heaven on earth and can only be reached by water. Originally inhabited by the Waccamaw Indians before Europeans sailed to shore, today it is used as an educational research facility for the marine science department of Coastal Carolina University. It can be explored by the public—but it's best to have a pro guide you to stay ahead of the rising and falling tides. I recommend the folks at Great Escapes Kayak Expeditions for their three-hour, easy-paddle kayaking adventure for your family. Choose a single or double kayak and follow the lead of one of their trained pros through the marsh channels that lead to Waties Island, where you may spot bottlenose dolphins, loggerhead sea turtles, blue herons, osprey, and more. And, while on the island, you can shell, swim, or sunbathe!

1116 Hwy. 9 E, Longs, 843-241-4588
greatescapeskayak.com

57

CHEER ON
CCU ATHLETICS

While Myrtle Beach isn't technically a college town, our pride and joy is Coastal Carolina University (CCU), home of the Chanticleers. (It's a Geoffrey Chaucer reference to a "proud and fierce rooster.") Depending on when you're in town, it's worth a visit to campus to watch a game by this fiercely competitive school in the Sun Belt Conference. In the fall, book a ticket at Brooks Stadium for a football game on the teal turf. It's fun to watch a team that has consistently won championships in the conference, has gone to bowl games, has been nationally ranked, and had players drafted into the NFL. In the spring, reserve your seat at Springs Brooks Stadium, where the baseball team reigns over the diamond. The underdog team won the College World Series in 2016 and continues to put on an impressive show. (I'm a CCU alum, but I promise I'm not biased.) Chants up!

100 Chanticleer Dr., Conway, 843-347-3161
coastal.edu

SWING LIKE A PRO
AT HAWAIIAN RUMBLE MINIGOLF

Did you know that Myrtle Beach is known among the mini golf elite as the "Mini Golf Capital of the World"? In fact, the US ProMiniGolf Association (USPMGA) holds its annual Master's three-day tourney at the Hawaiian Rumble Minigolf course in North Myrtle Beach for a cash purse of $25,000. Don't worry, most of us aren't that serious about mini golf—or "putt putt" as they call it around here—and there are more than 50 mini golf courses in the area to take a swing at. But Hawaiian Rumble is ranked number one in the world by the USPMGA, so these are hallowed grounds covering 18 holes. The course is themed around a tropical Hawaiian garden, with the centerpiece a massive 40-foot volcano in the middle. As you meander your way around the challenging obstacles, tune into relaxing Hawaiian music to truly transport you to the islands.

3210 Hwy. 17 S, North Myrtle Beach, 843-272-7812
hawaiianrumbleminigolf.com

59

RESERVE A TEE TIME
AT ANY OF MYRTLE BEACH'S 90 GOLF COURSES

Also renowned as the "Golf Capital of the World," Myrtle Beach hosts more than 90 championship golf courses designed for all skill levels, so it's hard to narrow to one—or even a few top choices—because we have more courses consistently ranked in *Golfweek*'s "Best of" list than any other golf destination in the country. I will advise you, however, to reserve a tee time or book a golf trip in the spring (March/April) or fall (October/early November), popular golf seasons that avoid the sultry summer heat. Recent exciting golf news was the announcement of the Myrtle Beach Classic, a new PGA TOUR event coming to the private Dunes Golf and Beach Club in May 2024. It will be the first PGA TOUR event in our local history and the first major professional golf tournament here in the past 24 years.

1359 21st Ave. N, Myrtle Beach, 843-477-8822
myrtlebeachgolfpassport.com

SADDLE UP AND GO HORSEBACK RIDING ON THE BEACH

In the beach's off-season—late November through late February—horseback riding is welcome on the sand and in the surf of our coastline, when swimmers and sunbathers are huddled indoors and nowhere to be found. It's fun this time of year to take a stroll and spy the imprints of horses' hooves in the soft sand. Horseback Riding of Myrtle Beach, a horse farm in Conway, offers gentle, sure-footed horses and highly trained equestrian guides for a safe, scenic beach ride that will refresh your spirit. No prior riding experience is necessary, and the group that you ride in will stay close together, but the guides encourage you to ride at the pace that feels most comfortable, from a slow walk to a medium trot. All horses are calm enough to be led into the water for a little splash. At the end of the tour, a disc of pics is yours free of charge.

4800 Johnson Shelly Rd., Conway, 843-997-1876
myrtlebeachhorserides.com

STAND UP ON A PADDLEBOARD IN THE INLET

Stand-up paddleboarding (SUP) is not only a great balancing workout for your body's core, but a sublime way to glide through the water and see our coastal surroundings from a unique perspective. My husband and I tend to launch our boards in the inlet at Morse Landing Park, where there's little to no water traffic (and he'll sometimes take a wave in with his SUP in the ocean), but there are many inlets, marshes, lakes, and rivers to SUP in our area. If you're a beginner, try Jack's Surf Lessons to learn the fundamentals from a top-notch instructor. Jack's also offers semiprivate, two-hour tours of the river and the inlet at sunrise, sunset, or anytime; you'll learn about some of South Carolina's most diverse coastal wildlife as you're paddling away.

3200 S Ocean Blvd., Myrtle Beach, 843-647-7471
jackssurflessons.com

TAKE A BOAT
TO THE POINT OR SANDY ISLAND

Two go-to spots to anchor for local boaters in the summer are The Point in Murrells Inlet or Sandy Island off the Intracoastal Waterway. You can only get to these two secluded beaches by boat, which are perfect for swimming, playing, and exploring. The Point is a stretch of beach where the inlet and the ocean meet, between the south of Garden City and the jetties that border the north end of Huntington Beach State Park. The kids can wade and splash in the calm waters while you set up camp on the sand. Sandy Island, a hidden sandbar tucked beyond narrow channels that turn off the Waccamaw River and the Great Pee Dee, is steeped in history. The island is owned by the Nature Conservancy, which oversees the 9,000-acre wildlife preserve. It's home to about 50 descendants of enslaved Africans, who used to work the rice plantations on the island. The island's children today still take a ferry to the mainland to school each day.

Beach House Boat Rentals
Wacca Wache Marina or Dead Dog Saloon Dock, Murrells Inlet, 843-882-5210
beachhouseboatrentals.com

Crazy Sister Marina
4123 US 17 Business, Murrells Inlet, 843-651-3676
crazysistermarina.com

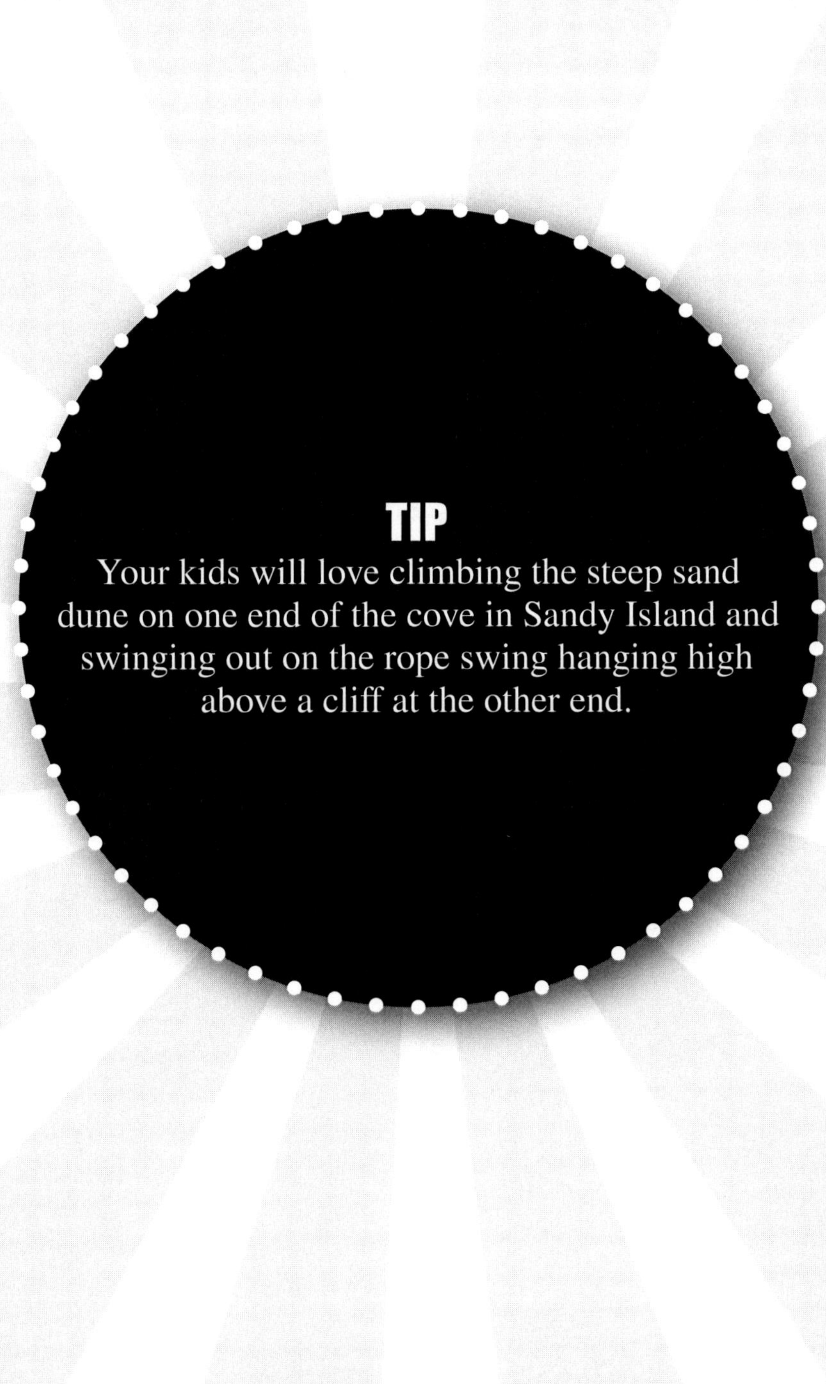

TIP

Your kids will love climbing the steep sand dune on one end of the cove in Sandy Island and swinging out on the rope swing hanging high above a cliff at the other end.

63

TAKE TO THE OPEN SEA
ON A JET SKI

In tandem with the major influx of people migrating to live in this hot real estate market are the number of boats flooding our local waters that new homeowners are buying. This boat traffic then tends to cram and crowd the river. Which is why, if you have the need for speed and want to hop on a Jet Ski, rent one from Downwind Sails Watersports, which offers the only Jet Ski rentals on the ocean in Myrtle Beach. For 30 minutes, crank up the Jet Ski and skim across the water in Downwind's triangular course, which is about 150 yards between each point. Downwind is a trusted, locally owned company that's been renting out Jet Skis, catamaran sailboats, and kayaks, and running banana boat rides and parasailing, since 1978.

410 S Ocean Blvd., Myrtle Beach, 843-236-7245
2985 S Ocean Blvd., Myrtle Beach, 843-448-7245
downwindsailsmyrtlebeach.com

Dress water-appropriate because you will get wet! It's also a good idea to wear corded sunglasses to protect your eyes from the water spray when you're speeding along. And wear flip-flops or water shoes down to the shoreline where you will launch because the sand is hot!

TAKE SURF LESSONS
WITH VILLAGE SURF SHOPPE

Spreading stoke since 1969, Village Surf Shoppe has been a Myrtle Beach surfers' staple, from groms to pros. Sitting on Atlantic Avenue before you cross the causeway to the Garden City Pier, Village is the longest-running surf shop in the area, and today run by Kelly Richards, who had his time on the national surf circuit and has since passed the talents down to son, Cam Richards, who is currently ranked 15th in the World Surfer League. While Kelly spends most of his time shaping his Perfection surfboards at the shop during the day, his crew stays busy guiding students young and old on how to surf in either private or group camp lessons. Just sign up and meet at the Calhoun Drive Beach Access on Garden City Beach and they will take great care of you. You'll be popping up and catching a wave in no time!

500 Atlantic Ave., Murrells Inlet, 843-651-6396
villagesurfshoppe.com

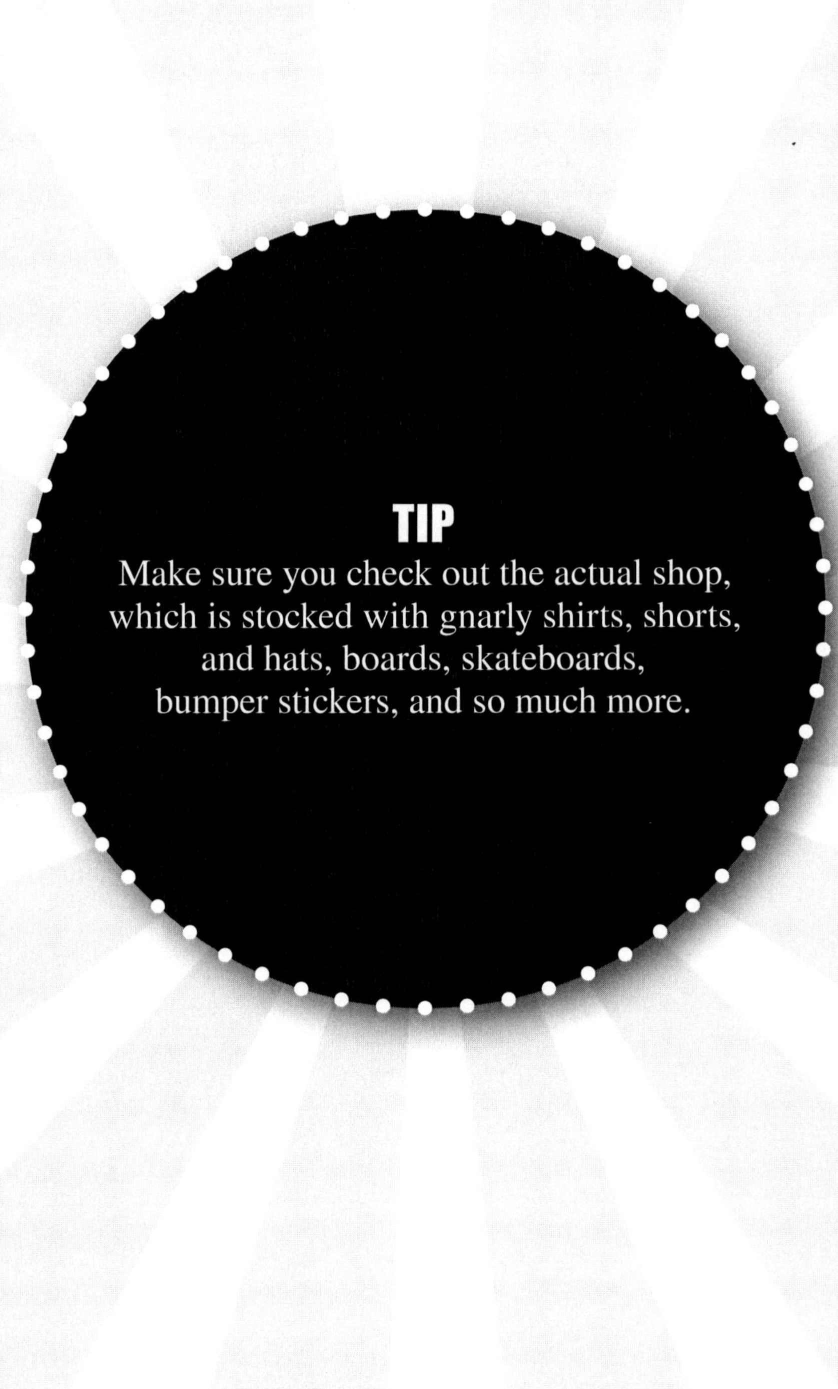

TIP

Make sure you check out the actual shop, which is stocked with gnarly shirts, shorts, and hats, boards, skateboards, bumper stickers, and so much more.

SCUBA DIVE
DOWN TO HISTORIC SHIPWRECKS AND ARTIFICIAL REEFS

The waters along the Myrtle Beach coast are just begging to be discovered below their surface, and scuba diving is the best way to do it. No matter your skill level, you're in good hands with the pro team at Coastal Scuba, who instructs beginners as young as 8 years old in the pool to advanced open-water diving classes to PADI master diving. Exciting scuba dive sites include the *Sherman*, a 140-year-old, post–Civil War blockade runner that sunk in 52 feet of water about six miles from the Little River inlet that features overwhelming marine life, plus possible treasures, like old US military belt buckles and buttons. A bounty of cool artificial reefs include Barracuda Alley, a former 150-foot barge with concrete piping and steel A-frames and 20 armored personnel carriers nestled 10 miles off the coast, and the Bill Perry, sunk in the 1990s as part of the South Carolina Artificial Reef Program.

1903 Hwy. 17 S, North Myrtle Beach, 843-361-3323
coastalscuba.com

SIT COURTSIDE
AT THE BEACH BALL CLASSIC

Tipping off right before and after Christmas, the Beach Ball Classic (BBC), held at the Myrtle Beach Convention Center, has been a holiday tradition since former NBA coach (and local high school basketball coach) Dan D'Antoni founded it in 1981. This ultimate high school basketball tournament draws the best in the sport from across the country—even into Canada. Games run all day and are so action-packed that you won't believe players are at the high school level. And when I say the best in the sport, I mean that it's a feeding ground for NBA prospects. Former BBC players who launched their career include Kobe Bryant, Grant Hill, Vince Carter, Kevin Garnett, Baron Davis, Jason Kidd, Raymond Felton, and Rasheed Wallace, to name a few.

2101 N Oak St., Myrtle Beach, 843-918-1225
myrtlebeachconventioncenter.com

GO SHELLING

ON A BARRIER ISLAND IN GEORGETOWN

Hop aboard Cap'n Rod's Lowcountry Boat Tour, a 56-foot pontoon boat docked at Front Street in Georgetown, and take a ride along the river and channels leading to Winyah Bay on one of their most popular tours: the Lighthouse Shell Island Tour. En route to the unspoiled barrier island, you'll pass by North Island, site of the oldest lighthouse in continuous operation in South Carolina, where the legend of Lighthouse Annie lives on. It's said that, in the 1800s, the lighthouse keeper and his young daughter, Annie, got caught in a furious storm on the way back to the island from Georgetown and drowned. Today, she warns sailors to go back ahead of bad storms. After you beach on the island, you'll have an hour and a half to search for shells, beachcomb, or take a deep breath of fresh air and relax in peace.

701 Front St., Georgetown, 843-477-0287
lowcountrytours.com

TIP

Make sure you bring a bag or bucket to gather all your shell finds.

TAKE A WALK
ON THE MYRTLE BEACH BOARDWALK

The oceanfront Myrtle Beach Boardwalk and Promenade gives you 1.2 miles to walk from the 14th Avenue to Second Avenue Piers—and shop, eat, and play along the way. The boardwalk itself is a beauty, laid out with wider sections and more narrow walkways lined with lush, tropical landscaping. Be sure to take the kids to Fun Plaza, an open-air arcade offering vintage coin games, Skee-Ball, and more. Every Friday over the summer, free seaside concerts—from classic rock to reggae—take place in Plyler Park next to the SkyWheel and around the large bronze sculpture, *Goddess of the Sea*. Pick up a souvenir at any of the shops, and when it's time to refuel, get some ice cream at Mad Myrtle's Ice Creamery or a bite to eat at the Pier House Restaurant on the pier or 8th Ave. Tiki Bar & Grill.

1st Ave. N to 16th Ave. N, Myrtle Beach
myrtlebeachdowntown.com

69

FLY AND CLIMB
ON ZIP LINES AND ROPES COURSES

There are a handful of zip lines and ropes courses in our area that will give you a bird's-eye view of the coastal grounds below. Myrtle Beach Zip Line Adventures glides across the oceanfront lawn where the Pavilion once stood toward the ocean, with a Ninja Kids Course for the wee ones and Aerial Challenge Courses for older climbers. Soar + Explore zips 50 feet above Lake Broadway for 1,000 feet between two towers and features a tropical-themed ropes course. Radical Ropes Adventure Park will have you swinging, climbing, and zipping through the trees of a forest. The aerial course features three levels that soar up to 55 feet above ground level. For an extra challenge, climb their massive outdoor climbing wall and then free-fall down 70 feet on the other side.

Myrtle Beach Zip Line Adventures
321 9th Ave N, Myrtle Beach, 843-839-1661
mbziplines.com

Soar + Explore
1313 Celebrity Cir., Myrtle Beach, 843-626-9962
wonderworksonline.com/myrtle-beach/the-experience/soar-explore

Radical Ropes Adventure Park
301 19th Ave. S, Myrtle Beach, 843-723-4225
radicalropes.com

70

GO FLY A KITE

AT THE KLIG'S KITES KITE FESTIVAL

Once or twice a year, you can look up at the sky and witness an amazing spectacle of hundreds of kites of all shapes and sizes dancing in the ocean breeze above the beach. Klig's Kites is the go-to place for kites and flags in town (two locations), and owner Richard Kligman loves to celebrate his passion with the community through these festivals. The all-day, two-day events rotate locales on the Myrtle Beach coastline each year, but you can always expect them to be family-friendly, with food, drinks, and kites available to purchase, and professional kite flyers on-site giving demos and teaching people how to fly two-string and four-string kites. Expect to see delta kites, diamond kites, sled kites, parafoil kites, and beginner through quad line and power stunt and trick kites at the festival.

1215 Celebrity Cir., Myrtle Beach, 843-448-7881
4505 Hwy. 17 S, North Myrtle Beach, 843-448-7881
kligs.com

TIP

If you miss out on the kite festival, stop by either of the Klig's Kites shop locations above to purchase a kite and fly it on your own any day on the beach.

Myrtle Beach Art Museum

CULTURE AND HISTORY

BROWSE ART
AT THE MYRTLE BEACH ART MUSEUM

The Myrtle Beach Art Museum, technically the Burroughs-Chapin Art Museum, is a haven for the arts for all ages! March up the mural-painted front steps into this 1920s beach bungalow and discover a cultural palette of the visual arts here at the beach. Browse through their unique traveling national exhibitions in all media formats that change up every few months, as well as their four collections of art: the Waccamaw Arts and Crafts Guild Collection, the Burgess-Dinkelspiel Collection of Southern Art, the Bishop Collection of Antique Maps & Historical Prints, and the Gifts & Purchases Collection. Also, take advantage of their interactive educational programs, from classes for kids and youth to pottery classes for adults. Don't worry, this isn't a total hands-off art museum for kiddos. There are art and craft play areas here and there to keep them busy.

3100 S Ocean Blvd., Myrtle Beach, 843-238-2510
myrtlebeachartmuseum.org

TOUR
THROUGH AN OCEANFRONT CASTLE

New York City power couple Archer and Anna Huntington built Atalaya Castle between 1931 and 1933 as their winter residence. Situated oceanfront amid coastal vegetation within Huntington Beach State Park, the castle was designed by Archer himself to mimic Spanish or Moorish architecture, with his own spin, including the wrought iron grills on all the windows for hurricane protection and a 40-foot-tall water tower in the center of the courtyard. Atalaya means "watchtower" in Spanish. Today, you can take a fascinating guided tour of the 30 rooms that surround three sides of the courtyard, including indoor and outdoor art studios for Anna and a room with animal enclosures, where the couple kept bears, horses, monkeys, and a leopard. Archer died in 1955 and Anna last visited Atalaya in 1958. Atalaya Castle was placed on the National Register of Historic Places in 1984.

Huntington Beach State Park, Atalaya Rd., Murrells Inlet, 843-237-4440
atalayacastle.com

TIP

This is a popular backdrop for wedding, graduation, and family portraits, so you may want to bring your camera to capture some special pics, too.

73

STOP AND SMELL THE ROSES AT BROOKGREEN GARDENS

Once four thriving rice plantations, Brookgreen Gardens today has bloomed into a nationally recognized blend of art, nature, and history. Archer Huntington, New York City native and one of the wealthiest men in America, bought the property in 1930 as a retreat for his wife, successful sculptor Anna Hyatt Huntington, who had been diagnosed with tuberculosis. A year later, Brookgreen was incorporated as a private nonprofit. Today, the 9,127-acre preserve is the first (and largest) public sculpture garden in the country, like a rare, hybrid outdoor museum. Highlights are the Live Oak Allee lined with 250-year-old live oaks, the Brenda W. Rosen Carolina Terrace Garden bursting with perennials and roses, the Palmetto Garden featuring the playful Fountain of the Muses, and the 2,000-plus sculptures by over 400 artists scattered throughout the garden.

1931 Brookgreen Dr., Murrells Inlet, 843-235-6000
brookgreen.org

Visit Brookgreen Gardens over the holidays for their amazing Nights of a Thousand Candles event, when the gardens and paths glow with nearly 3,000 hand-lit candles and millions of sparkling lights, and the sounds of holiday music are in the air.

PLAY YOUR HEART OUT
AT THE MYRTLE BEACH PINBALL MUSEUM

Blast to your 1970s, '80s, and '90s past at this unique museum that features more than 26 retro pinball machines for your playing pleasure. It all started out of the husband-and-wife owners' personal collection and, over the years, grew to become South Carolina's largest collection of pinball machines for the public to see and play. It's an all-volunteer gig for the group of pinball enthusiasts, who only want to share their passion for the lost art form and preserve and promote this important part of American pop culture for younger generations. Here's how it works: admission is $12 per hour, per person, and reservations need to be made online in advance because of limited capacity. Once you buy your ticket and arrive at the museum, all pinball games are set on "Free Play," so no quarters, coins, or tokens are needed!

607 27th Ave. N, Myrtle Beach, 843-282-9018
myrtlebeachpinballmuseum.org

SEE OUR STATE'S GREATS
AT THE SOUTH CAROLINA HALL OF FAME

Located within the halls of the Myrtle Beach Convention Center, the South Carolina Hall of Fame was signed into law as the state's official Hall of Fame by South Carolina Governor Jim Hodges on September 21, 2001. With inductees trailing as far back as the 18th century, the hall of fame honors past and contemporary citizens of South Carolina who made notable contributions to our state's heritage and progress. One living and one deceased inductee may be named each year. Meander up and down the walls of photos and plaques of facts to learn more about South Carolina's pride and joy, including Bernard Baruch; Pat Conroy; Ronald Erwin McNair, PhD; Bobby Richardson; and Strom Thurmond. Most recent inductees are multiplatinum recording artist Darius Rucker; Dr. Leo Twiggs, an artist, educator, and museum director; and the late Elizabeth Evelyn Wright, founder of the Denmark Industrial Institute.

2101 N Oak St., Myrtle Beach, 843-626-7444
theofficialschalloffame.com

TIP

Take the quiz online (easy, moderate, and difficult levels) to test your knowledge of South Carolina.

TRAVEL BACK IN TIME
AT THE HORRY COUNTY MUSEUM

Myrtle Beach is in Horry (pronounced O-ree) County, and the impressive Horry County Museum in Conway celebrates the history of one of the largest counties in the Eastern United States. Tour the two-story brick building that was first established in 1981 and later opened its doors in the museum's current location in a historic, renovated school building in historic downtown Conway in 2014, and learn the history, natural history, and culture of our county. Take in all the exhibits, including a freshwater aquarium that was featured on Animal Planet's *Tanked*, and view one of their presentations in the 600-seat auditorium. The museum's L.W. Paul Living History Farm nearby is also worth a visit, where they recreate life on a one-horse family farm that would have been common in the area between 1900 and 1955.

805 Main St., Conway, 843-915-5320
horrycountymuseum.org

Make a day of it in downtown Conway, which is home to several foodie-credible restaurants, such as Rivertown Bistro, the Trestle Cafe, and Hop N' Wich. Then, take the time to find all nine murals painted on the historic buildings throughout town.

LEARN ABOUT GEORGETOWN'S RICE HISTORY AT THE RICE MUSEUM

In the late 1700s, rice reigned as the chief commodity crop in Georgetown in the antebellum era. Rice plantation owners quickly became aristocrats, and the county was reported as the wealthiest per capita in the former colonies as of 1840, thanks to the port exporting the most rice of any port in the world. The Rice Museum, housed in the Town Clock on Front Street, has spilled out of its small space over the last 50-plus years to include a unique gift shop and a gallery collection of curated local artists. The main 45-minute tour covers the colorful rice culture of Georgetown and goes over the Brown's Ferry vessel on-site, the oldest types of colonial manufacturing in the country, and other exhibits. Sign up for a special program; a good one is the "Art of Indigo Dyeing" workshop.

633 Front St., Georgetown, 843-546-7423
ricemuseum.org

WITNESS SOUTHERN LIVING
AT THE KAMINSKI HOUSE MUSEUM

The Kaminski House Museum in historic Georgetown was once home to some of the most successful businessmen in the South, like the original builder of the house, Paul Trapier, known as "The King of Georgetown," and Heiman Kaminski, father of Harold Kaminski, the owner of the Kaminski House. The museum today opens its doors to visitors to tour the fabulous architecture and antique pieces, witness the meticulously preserved estate, and bask in what was Georgetown living in the 18th century. There are more than 60 antebellum homes throughout Georgetown, but the Kaminski House best reflects the Georgian style of that era. It's quite the beauty, built on a bluff that overlooks the Sampit River, site of many summer concerts and weddings on the lawn today. Your guided tour will weave through the rooms and spin the historic tales as if the walls could talk.

1003 Front St., Georgetown, 843-546-7706
kaminskimuseum.org

79

DISCOVER THE RICH HISTORY
OF HOBCAW BARONY

Hobcaw Barony gets its name from the Native American word *hobcaw*, which means "between the waters." It's a 16,000-acre research reserve on the Waccamaw Neck off Winyah Bay. The history of Hobcaw Barony has evolved quite a bit over the years, from becoming an official colonial land grant, or barony, in 1718 to being sold and subdivided into rice plantations through the early 20th century to being purchased by Bernard M. Baruch, a Wall Street financier who rubbed elbows with presidents, in 1905 for a hunting retreat. Fifty years later, Bernard sold the entire property to his daughter, Belle Baruch, who created the Belle Baruch Foundation before she died in 1964. The foundation today manages the land as an outdoor lab for colleges in South Carolina. You can take a two-hour guided tour of Bernard's 1930s home, which has hosted the likes of Winston Churchill and President Franklin Roosevelt; the home and stables of Bellefield Plantation; the Discovery Center; and one of four slave villages.

22 Hobcaw Rd., Georgetown, 843-546-4623
hobcawbarony.org

IMMERSE YOURSELF IN HISTORY

AT THE SOUTH CAROLINA MARITIME MUSEUM

Founded in 2011, the South Carolina Maritime Museum, appropriately located waterfront on Georgetown's Front Street, celebrates the layers of maritime history immersed in the state and Georgetown, South Carolina's second-largest port. Photographs, documents, artifacts, and interactive exhibits bring to life the stories behind South Carolina's port cities of Georgetown, Charleston, and Beaufort, as well as the intricate network of inland waterways. Learn more about the Fresnel lens of the old North Island lighthouse; Lafayette's first arrival in the United States from France at a resort on North Island aboard *La Victoire* in 1777; Georgetown's fishing industry, including caviar, shrimp, oysters, crabs, and game fish; the 1865 sinking of the USS *Harvest Moon* in Winyah Bay, the only flagship lost by Union soldiers during the Civil War; and more.

729 Front St., Georgetown, 843-520-0111
scmaritimemuseum.org

GET EDUCATED ON THE PAST

AT THE HISTORIC MYRTLE BEACH COLORED SCHOOL & EDUCATION CENTER

Originally opened in 1932, the Myrtle Beach Colored School educated African American students in the Myrtle Beach area during those segregated times for more than 20 years. The school was a source of pride for the African American community. But after the Carver Training School opened in 1953, the schoolhouse was no longer in use, became dilapidated, and would have to be razed because of a city road-widening project. Fast-forward to 2006, when donations from city and county officials and grants made it possible for the Historic Myrtle Beach Colored School Museum and Education Center to be built less than two blocks from the original schoolhouse. Today, the facility displays artifacts from the school and time period and offers a poignant look into the past and a reference library of African American history, plus provides educational programs.

900 Dunbar St., 843-918-4905
cityofmyrtlebeach.com

TAKE A DRIVE DOWN MEMORY LANE AT WHEELS OF YESTERYEAR

The Myrtle Beach area isn't just known for our 60 miles of beach, but also for putting on some mileage around a racetrack. The former Myrtle Beach Speedway hosted the NASCAR Cup Series from 1958 to 1965, with a few greats taking the track to train, like Jeff Gordon, all four generations of Pettys, and three generations of Earnhardts. The Wheels of Yesteryear Vintage Auto Museum, located right by the old speedway, is a pit-stop must when you're in town. The museum, open since 2009, showcases more than 150 American-made classic and muscle cars and trucks. It's a beautiful collection that has been 55 years in the making by longtime car enthusiast Paul Cummings and his wife, Carol. In addition to the car stars of the show, Wheels of Yesteryear's gift shop is stocked with their logoed apparel, licensed brand hats and T-shirts, diecast metal signs, vintage collectibles, and car art.

413 Hospitality Ln., Myrtle Beach, 843-903-4774
facebook.com/wheelsofyesteryear

RIDE ON A TROLLEY
FOR A MYRTLE BEACH HISTORY TOUR

Step aboard an enclosed, climate-controlled trolley in front of the movie theater in The Market Common and step back in time in one of several themed two-hour Myrtle Beach history tours on different days of the week. On Tuesdays, it's "Myrtle Beach History, Movies, and Music," as your friendly guide, Kathryn Hedgepath, tells you the story of Myrtle Beach's role in the movies that were made and premiered here and in music history, with stops including the Fitzgerald Motel at Charlie's Place historic site from *Green Book*. Wednesday's "Early Myrtle Beach History and the WWII Years" tour explores U-boat threats off the coast. Thursday's "Myrtle Beach Area Ghosts, Pirates and Historic Families" tour explores Murrells Inlet and Pawleys Island, and on select Fridays, the "Myrtle Beach Military History Trolley Tour" includes a catered reception to conclude things at Tupelo Honey.

4002 Deville St., Myrtle Beach, 843-446-7824
myrtle-beach-history-tours.business.site

SEE A GHOST AFTER DINNER
AT THE BRENTWOOD

The historic Brentwood Restaurant & Wine Bistro in Little River is a phenomenal venue known for its French cuisine and serving a helping of "spirits." Brentwood's three-course dinner and ghost tour, with dinner starting at 7 p.m. and the tour kicking off after dessert, is a popular event. Storytellers will guide you through the house, narrating the history and ghost sightings. The Victorian-era home dates back to 1910. Ghost sightings by witnesses have been rampant over the years, such as a dark, fast shadow that passes several times by the upstairs bathroom into the front room and going through the upstairs fireplace; a face in the upstairs window that is supposedly Essie, the original owner, when no one is there; multiple orbs in digital photos; sighing voices in the walls; a small child appearing in the surveillance cameras; wine glasses falling off the tables; and more.

4269 Luck Ave., Little River, 843-249-2601
thebrentwoodrestaurant.com

85

SALUTE THE BRAVE
AT WARBIRD PARK

Warbird Park proudly stands on the grounds of the former Myrtle Beach Air Force Base on the outskirts of The Market Common and the Myrtle Beach International Airport. The Air Force base operated from the 1950s until March 1993. And today, the memorial Warbird Park is site of several old fighter planes: the A-10 Thunderbolt II, nicknamed "The Warthog," providing air support for troops during Operation Desert Storm; the F-100 Super Sabre, which was tasked with locating and destroying North Vietnamese enemy air defenses in the Vietnam War; and the LTV A-7 Corsair II, initially in service with the US Navy during the Vietnam War and later adopted, with some modifications, by the US Air Force. Warbird Park is also home to a 9/11 Memorial, a beam from the North Tower of the World Trade Center, as well as a Wall of Service and Circle of Heroes, and will soon showcase a new World War II memorial.

Farrow Pkwy., Myrtle Beach
facebook.com/warbirdpark

SEE SEAWORTHINESS
AT THE WOODEN BOAT SHOW

Touted as one of the Southeast's best wooden boat exhibits, the Georgetown Wooden Boat Show always closes down Front Street in Georgetown on the third weekend of October. Two full days are packed with activities, including a youth sailing regatta. The main wooden boat exhibit features more than 100 classic wooden boats that range in size from kayaks to yachts on display on the street and the water, and a wooden boatbuilding challenge for teams of two to build a rowing skiff in four hours and then test their boats for seaworthiness in a rowing relay race on the river. There are also knot-tying demos; kids' model boatbuilding; and maritime-related arts, crafts, and exhibits. And when you're ready for a break, the show also has a beer garden and food court, or you can explore all the shops and cafés along Front Street.

729 Front St., Georgetown, 843-520-0111
woodenboatshow.com

SIT BACK AND ENJOY THE SHOW
AT THE MYRTLE BEACH INTERNATIONAL FILM FESTIVAL

Lighting up the big screen for nearly 20 years, the Myrtle Beach International Film Festival (MBIFF) is held at the Grand 14 Movie Theatre in The Market Common. Filmmakers from around the world gather here in Myrtle Beach to premiere their works for ticket holders to the main event. Audience members, a mix of film fanatics, filmmakers, and industry professionals, will also be attending networking, forums, and more events offered by the MBIFF to give those in the industry a chance to seek out a collaborative partner or possible distribution deal. Short and full-length films are judged by a panel of seven. And stakes are high, because the festival is consistently recognized as a top festival with national and international awards, like the "Top 25 Film Festivals in the World to Submit To" by *MovieMaker* magazine. All you have to do is sit back and enjoy the show!

4002 Deville St., Myrtle Beach, 843-497-0220
myrtlebeachfilmfestival.com

FIND THE TUNNEL
UNDER OCEAN BOULEVARD

Yes, Myrtle Beach is below sea level, but that doesn't stop us from being on top of the tourism game—by digging a tunnel under Ocean Boulevard. It's a hidden treasure that's actually been around since the 1980s as the brainchild of a former owner of the Sea Mist Resort to serve as Myrtle Beach's only underground passage next to the property at 13th Avenue South and South Ocean Boulevard. Back in the '80s, there were four lanes and parking, with no real turn lanes or a median, but now there are two lanes and a turn lane, so this tunnel allowed pedestrians to safely cross the busy boulevard. The unmarked, must-see tunnel crosses under the busy Ocean Boulevard traffic in less than 100 yards. Along your walk, you'll love the under-the-sea colorful murals of dolphins and scuba divers on the walls and ceiling!

Ocean Blvd. and 13 Ave. S, Myrtle Beach
myrtlebeachseamist.com

THE
MARKET
COMMON
ESTATE · SALES / RENTALS

SHOPPING AND FASHION

GET FRESH
AT MYRTLE BEACH FARMERS MARKETS

Our Myrtle Beach coastline is known for fresh seafood and the best catches of the day served on the menus of a bounty of area restaurants, but we also offer a fair share of farmers markets selling fruits, veggies, and more each week in the summer and fall. Myrtle's Market in downtown Myrtle Beach features produce and handcrafted wares; the North Myrtle Beach Farmers Market has produce, jellies and jams, and baked goods; Valor Park Farmers Market in The Market Common has fresh produce, local seafood, treats, and artisan goods; and Surfside Farmers Market next to the library features local produce and seafood, canned and baked goods, flowers, and crafts. Expect about 20 farmers and vendors on hand at each market, with most events organized by the locally based Waccamaw Market Co-op.

Myrtle's Market
Corner of Mr. Joe White Ave. and Oak St., Myrtle Beach

North Myrtle Beach Farmers Market
925 1st Ave. S, North Myrtle Beach

Valor Park Farmers Market
1120 Farrow Pkwy., Myrtle Beach

Surfside Beach Farmers Market
Corner of Surfside and Willow Drives, Surfside Beach

Little River Farmers Market
4460 Mineola Ave., Little River

International Culinary Institute of Myrtle Beach
920 Crabtree Ln., Myrtle Beach

Georgetown Farmers Market
122 Screven St., Georgetown

SPEND A LAYOVER IN ASIA SHOPPING
AT FUDI MART

Travel to Asia without needing a passport at Fudi Mart in Surfside Beach, one of the best international grocers in our area at some of the most affordable prices. The large former Chinese food buffet building is now lined with rows of shelves neatly stocked with tons of foods and products from East and Southeast Asia. Aside from a shopping trip, it's practically a hybrid field trip of discovery and learning experience! Expect a wide variety of canned, packaged, frozen, and fresh foods, such as meat, fish, and produce, including homemade kimchi. There are loads of ramen noodle and rice noodle options, rice, sauces, seasonings, wontons, sushi wraps, pork buns, sweets, teas, sake, and so much more to explore. And if you don't know what a product is, ask the attentive staff!

901 Business 17 N, Surfside Beach, 843-213-1918
facebook.com/fudimart

STROLL UNDER THE LIVE OAKS AT THE HAMMOCK SHOPS

The historic Hammock Shops Village, sprawled out under the live oaks of Pawleys Island, has kept up with the trends in style and fashion. The past is in the village's moniker, which is based on the "Original Hammock Shop" that opened in 1938, where the hammock was first created and still sold here today. A prominent riverboat captain ferrying rice and supplies between Georgetown and Waverly Mills in 1889 designed a hammock for cooler, more breathable sleeping on the boat using cotton ropes woven without any thick knots. The result impacted the economy and symbolized the relaxing culture of the island. Today, this namesake's outdoor shopping complex features 23 unique boutiques and shops—from jewelry to apparel to gifts and more—two restaurants, a central playground, common places, and lush landscaping.

10880 Ocean Hwy., Pawleys Island
hammockshopsvillage.com

92

SHOP UPTOWN
AT THE MARKET COMMON

On the grounds of the former Air Force base, The Market Common opened in April 2008. The mixed-use, open-air destination for living, dining, shopping, and entertainment is charming in a Main Street USA way, with fountains, play areas, and tree-lined streets named after Air Force heroes who had trained here going back to World War II. There are quite a few upscale, national chain stores in The Market Common, like Anthropologie and Pottery Barn, but also local unique boutiques, like the Seacoast Artists Gallery, featuring more than 70 local artists' original works in all media. Two Brothers Wood Works sells handcrafted wood furnishings and gifts. Manifest Design is a home designer's dream, and my favorite, Bijuju, is a trendy shop filled with cute and affordable clothing, jewelry, and accessories from head to toe.

4017 Deville St., Myrtle Beach, 843-839-3500
marketcommonmb.com

FIND IT ALL
AT BOULINEAU'S

Laid out in over four blocks in the Cherry Grove section of North Myrtle Beach, with two floors and more than 175,000 square feet of retail shopping, Boulineau's is a grocery store on steroids and one of the most unique in the country. Located one block from the oceanfront, it was first opened as a small grocery store by Frank and Louise Boulineau in 1948, when the Cherry Grove Beach community had fewer than 100 houses. Today you could get lost in here, but I'll try to map it out: there is fresh produce, Frank's fresh local seafood section that steams the fish for free, a meat department that includes their homemade sausages, groceries, a bakery, an ice cream shop, a deli, a café with oceanfront seating, and an entire floor of beach supplies, souvenirs, gifts, games, toys, fishing tackle, housewares, small appliances, and more.

212 Sea Mountain Hwy., North Myrtle Beach, 843-249-3556
boulineaus.com

BE A TOURIST
AT BEACH STORES

I know it seems kitschy and touristy, but whether it's for a want or a need, you really need to make your way to any of the oodles of beach stores we have in Myrtle Beach on just about every block. You'll find it all for the beach at these stores, from the necessary supplies and suits to toys, towels, footwear, and coolers. And you can pick up a souvenir with Myrtle Beach written on anything from head to toe, plus gifts and accessories. Here are some of my top local beach store picks: Eagles Beachwear, open since 1981 and now with about 20 locations in the area; Whales Beachwear & Resortwear, with multiple locations; Bargain Beachwear; I Love MB Resortwear; Tsunami Surf Shop; Pacific Superstore; and Jaws Resortwear in Murrells Inlet, which you can't miss with its massive shark mouth store entrance.

Eagles Beachwear
Multiple locations
eaglesbeachwear.net

Whales Beachwear & Resortwear
Multiple locations, 843-444-4300

Bargain Beachwear
Multiple locations, 843-497-2200

I Love MB Resortwear
2307 S Kings Hwy., Myrtle Beach, 843-808-9789
facebook.com/iheartmb1

Tsunami Surf Shop
Multiple locations
tsunamisurfshops.com

Pacific Superstore
Multiple locations
pacific-superstore5th.business.site

Jaws Resortwear
3055 US 17 Business, Murrells Inlet, 843-651-5956
facebook.com/jawsresortwear

95

SHARE A LEGACY
AT LEGACY ANTIQUES & CONSIGNMENTS

Drive south on 17 Business toward Murrells Inlet and you can't miss the cheerful, bright turquoise building on the right that houses Legacy Antiques & Consignments. Founded in 1988 by Judi Abbott, the store is truly a legacy because Abbott passed it down to her son, Sierra Abbott, and his wife, Arielle, in 2019. The couple is helpful and knowledgeable, and you will love scouring all the finds in the 10,000-square-foot space that's thoughtfully displayed with merchandising expertise, such as one-of-a-kind jewelry, antique furniture and accent pieces, lamps, art, wall art, and rugs. It's not all just fancy antiques—some treasures are funky, interesting conversation pieces. They also welcome consigners to add to their inventory for a fee. Overall, the goal is to pass on history by bringing the past into the present, and to have folks fall in love with something as a legacy to be shared.

3420 US 17 Business, Murrells Inlet, 843-651-0884
legacyantiques.net

GET A POP OF COLOR
AT PINK & RED

Here in the coastal South, we embrace a wardrobe of bright colors and floral prints, which is exactly what Pink & Red exudes in their inventory, as a Lilly Pulitzer Signature store in Myrtle Beach. The friendly neighborhood boutique opened its double doors on May 1, 2021. In addition to a large selection of Lilly Pulitzer, Pink & Red also specializes in women-owned brands that are headquartered in the South, such as Emily McCarthy, Julie Vos, Loren Hope, Briton Court, and Brianna Cannon. Women's and kids' options include tops, dresses, bottoms, rompers and jumpsuits, swimwear, activewear, sleepwear, jewelry, bags, and hair and lifestyle accessories, plus home, gift, and toy items. Another tradition in the South is monogramming, which is a service Pink & Red offers customized on just about anything for their clients.

5900 N Kings Hwy., Myrtle Beach, 843-839-3571
shoppinkandred.com

97

ADD TO YOUR COLLECTION
AT ART IN THE PARK

Organized by the Waccamaw Arts & Crafts Guild, one of the oldest art guilds in the area, Art in the Park (AITP) is held outdoors in Valor Park within The Market Common three weekends a year (April, October, and November). The popular all-day show and sale has been setting up this festival since 1972 in various locales in Myrtle Beach, welcoming artists and craftsmen from across the country to sell their original works in a variety of mediums. The kinds of visual art available here can include painting, sculpture, woodworking, photography, jewelry, fabric, glass, metal, pottery, stone, and mixed media. Don't worry, there's something for everyone at AITP! And when you need to take a break from shopping, the event usually has food and drink vendors on hand—or you can choose from any of the restaurants at The Market Common.

1120 Farrow Pwy., Myrtle Beach
wacg.org

MORE AREA ART FESTIVALS

Atalaya Arts & Crafts Festival
Huntington Beach State Park
16148 Ocean Hwy., Murrells Inlet, 843-237-4440
southcarolinaparks.com/huntington-beach

Blessing of the Inlet
Belin Memorial United Methodist Church
4182 US 17 Business, Murrells Inlet
belinumc.org

Craftsmen's Summer Classic Art & Craft Festival
Myrtle Beach Convention Center
2101 N Oak St., Myrtle Beach, 843-918-1225
gilmoreshows.com

Brookgreen Gardens Art Festival
1931 Brookgreen Dr., Murrells Inlet, 843-235-6000
brookgreen.org

SHOP 'TIL YOU DROP
AT HUDSON'S SURFSIDE FLEA MARKET

You'll need at least a couple of hours to comb through Hudson's Surfside Flea Market, the largest open-air market in the area. There's a lot of ground to cover, with several warehouses, 70,000 square feet, and more than 400 vendor spaces selling just about anything. Hudson's has been a family affair since Easter 1975, when patriarch Jack first built an antiques store out of an old log tobacco barn. Now it's operated by the third generation of Hudsons, Hayes and Josh. The shopping experience at Hudson's is a positive, friendly one—even award-winning, locally—featuring returning vendors with a mix of new ones selling antiques, golf supplies, jewelry, clothing, kitchenware, smartphone accessories, handmade goods, tools, trinkets, and so much more. Food and drinks are also served at Hudson's. For most of the year, Hudson's is open Thursdays through Sundays.

1040 US 17 Business, Surfside Beach, 843-238-0372
hudsonssurfsidefleamarket.com

GO FASHION-FORWARD
AT L. MAE BOUTIQUE AND WILD MABEL

Carolina pride is in full force at sister brands L. Mae Boutique and Wild Mabel Clothing Co. with boutique locations in Myrtle Beach and Pawleys Island. Owners are passionate about creating an artistic retail experience, with L. Mae giving off more colorful, preppy vibes and Wild Mabel considered more laid back and bohemian. They first started selling their fun, flirty, fashion-forward apparel online in 2012, and then their brick-and-mortar stores opened by popular demand. During football season, these stores are the headquarters for the cutest University of South Carolina or Clemson University ensembles. Either brand carries tops, blouses, tanks, sweaters and sweatshirts, maxi and short dresses, casual dresses, party dresses, shorts, skirts, denim, rompers, jumpers, jackets, vests, and loungewear. Accessories include jewelry, bags and totes, hair, hats, shoes, and socks. Lines in stock include Free People, MinkPink, Mumu, Spanx, THML, and Z Supply.

170 Sayebrook Pkwy., Myrtle Beach, 843-293-3515
myrtlebeach.lmaeboutique.com

GET LOST
AT THE GAY DOLPHIN

Step foot into the past at the landmark Gay Dolphin Gift Cove on the boardwalk, Myrtle Beach's oldest and largest gift shop. Owner Justin Plyler originally opened it as a small oceanfront shop in the 1940s, with a large amusement park for children. The name was chosen as one that is whimsical and inspired by the coastal location. It's a name that certainly is a memorable one today! Hurricane Hazel destroyed the Gay Dolphin in 1954, but the Plylers were resilient, rebuilding the store bigger and better than ever to feature the tall glass tower that still stands. The store today is 26,000 square feet in more than seven levels of shopping space. Sift through more than 70,000 items in stock, including seashells, Myrtle Beach souvenirs and apparel, collectibles, jewelry, toys, and sharks' teeth. Take a selfie at one of the seven photo opps, like the life-size Yeti, Elvis, or pirates.

916 N Ocean Blvd., Myrtle Beach, 843-448-6550
gaydolphin.com

Gay Dolphin
GIFT COVE

Little River Blue Crab Festival

ACTIVITIES
BY SEASON

SPRING

SUMMER

FALL

WINTER

CCU Athletics

Brookgreen Gardens

SUGGESTED
ITINERARIES

COUPLES

FAMILY-FRIENDLY

WATER LOVERS

HISTORY AND CULTURAL BUFFS

SPORTS AND REC

The Boathouse

INDEX

Myrtle Beach SkyWheel